ENGLISH POETRY

HOME STUDY BOOKS

HOME STUDY BOOKS
General Editor: B. Ifor Evans

ENGLISH POETRY

*The main currents
from Chaucer to the present*

by

DOUGLAS BUSH

METHUEN & CO. LTD., LONDON
36 Essex Street, Strand, W.C.2

First Published November 18, 1952
Reprinted with minor corrections 1961

.1.2

CATALOGUE NO. 2/4462/1

Reprinted by lithography and bound in Great Britain by
Jarrold and Sons Limited, Norwich

CONTENTS

INTRODUCTION

IN undertaking to survey the English poetry of six hundred years, from Chaucer to the present, in sixty thousand words, one could wish for the gift of succinctness displayed by Thomas Rymer—'Chaucer refin'd our English. Which in perfection by Waller.' England, or Great Britain, has been so rich in poetry that a multitude of writers on the lower levels have their measure of intrinsic value (not to mention those of mainly historical importance), but this small book must concentrate on the best. It does not, however, attempt to survey even the best poetry with the comprehensive and even-handed justice of a textbook, and it is not an aid for those whose minds are anxiously divided between poetry and examinations. It is in part an historical sketch, in part a reminder that the great poetry of all ages cannot grow old, a reminder of the sources of refreshment, humorous and tragic, aesthetic and religious, that have outlived many crises in the history of the race. Poetry is the distillation of man's experience in society and in solitude, of his joys and visions, his suffering and despair, his wisdom and fortitude, his efforts to grasp 'the burthen of the mystery'. It is because poetry is all of these things that in every age some people must write and read it, and that, while its spirit is always changing with changing experience in a changing world, great poetry nevertheless remains always alive and always 'true'. Poetry is also a fine art, since the best-intentioned poem is dead unless it is an aesthetic expression that evokes an aesthetic response. In technique and language, as in spirit, poetry renews its vitality through an inevitable and endless process of convention and revolt. The modern poet may recognize that Chaucer and Shakespeare and Milton are greater than any poet of recent times, but he could not possibly write in their way, even if he 'had the mind'. For the reader, however, there are no such barriers; all great poetry is, or may be, his present possession.

In such an essay as this, many fundamental things must be taken for granted or touched very briefly—changes in the physical and social conditions of life, in religious, philosophical, and scientific beliefs and doctrines, in the substance and structure of the language, in conceptions of the nature of poetry, in reactions to foreign literature and thought both ancient and modern. Many books could be and have been written on these subjects, and even in a small survey it would be possible to let poets and their works become only illustrations of this or that mixture of forces, traditions, and influences. But however important such external and internal factors are, we shall here be concerned with the individual poets and poems as they are in themselves rather than as products of their complex backgrounds.

On the other hand, while there are nowadays writers and readers who think that even the least pretentious approach to poetry should be purely or mainly aesthetic, formal, and technical, it is assumed here that the primary motives of both poets and their audience spring from their total sensibility and total experience. So far as this book has a continuous and unifying theme, it is that given by the poetry—

the varying impulses of poets towards the actual
and the ideal, the temporal and the eternal. If such
terms are vague and elusive, differences between the
two poles might be further suggested by 'Aristotelian' and 'Platonic', 'Apollonian' and 'Dionysian',
and of course 'classical' and 'romantic'.[1] Most of
the greater poets, while striving for wholeness and
order and unity, have been drawn in opposed
directions—that is one reason for their being the
greater poets. The individual writer's vision of order
may mean acceptance of the world or denial of the
world, acceptance of nature or denial of nature, or,
most often, inner conflicts that demand resolution.

No doubt it is chiefly since the rise of science and
the decline of religion that such conflicts have been
most common and acute. In the medieval poets,
who have a fuller spiritual—and artistic—security,
we see, not so much inner conflicts, but more or less
awareness of the gulf between the actual and the
ideal in a religious society. We see also the strength
of poetic convention, if not much revolt, and the
strength of native tradition, which can stand alone
(not that it itself is purely native) or can absorb
foreign influence and remain English.

[1] In the history and criticism of English poetry, this last
pair of words (which are more modern than the phenomena
they are applied to) have had a more fluid significance than
they have on the Continent, and suggest not merely antithesis but characteristically English continuity and compromise—as Sir B. Ifor Evans has shown at large in his
*Tradition and Romanticism: Studies in English Poetry from
Chaucer to Yeats* (1940).

Since a small book cannot carry notes or bibliography, grateful acknowledgement may be made here of the help derived
from the writings of innumerable scholars and critics.

Professors B. J. Whiting and H. E. Rollins have kindly
read parts of the proof.

CHAPTER I

THE MIDDLE AGES

FOR about two centuries after 1066, French was the language of the upper classes in England, English mainly the language of the lower; political conquest was naturally attended by linguistic and cultural conquest. But by the time of Chaucer's birth English had displaced French, English literature had established itself as against French and Latin (though it was much indebted to both), and Chaucer himself represented the emergence of individual writers from the forest of anonymity.

The special assimilation of French was not the only large factor in the development of English. The shift from an inflected to an uninflected speech worked drastic changes upon its very fibre. The extraordinary fluidity of Chaucer's verse is of course due in part to the syllabic value of the final *e* (though other poets who shared that common possession seldom got the same results). In later times, while some writers may have had an inkling of the truth, Chaucer was commonly thought—in Dryden's words—to have the rude sweetness of a Scotch tune; his scansion was not really understood until the middle of the nineteenth century. The poet whom Spenser looked back to as a 'well of English undefyled' was fortunate also in that his language was the dialect of the East Midlands and London which became modern English. Thus his original text gives little trouble to the uninstructed modern reader,

whereas the best contemporary poems—*Pearl*,
(which may be a richly symbolic elegy on a dead
child, though it has been interpreted in several other
ways), *Gawain and the Green Knight* (probably by the
same author), and the *Vision of Piers Plowman*—
were products of the alliterative revival of the North
Midlands and are more or less difficult; so far as these
have been read, it has been mainly in modernized
versions.

Geoffrey Chaucer (1340/43–1400) has remained the
unique poet of realistic acceptance and security; his
name is the very symbol of clear-eyed health and
sanity. He was, to be sure, a good Catholic in the
age of faith; the ultimate questions had been settled
for him and left him free to fix his ironic eye upon
the actualities of human nature and existence. Yet
if living in the age of faith were enough, there
would be no explanation for Wyclif and Langland,
and Chaucer's attitude towards life must be ascribed
largely to his own temperament and his background.
He was a man among men, an officer of the court and
a minor diplomat, a Comptroller of Customs and
Clerk of the King's Works, a justice of the peace and
a member of Parliament. He was at home in both
aristocratic and bourgeois worlds. And he was not
of course publishing books for the general public; he
wrote for himself and for the relatively small group
of people who shared his milieu and his tastes. We
could not expect him to have much sympathy with
'Jakke Straw and his meynee'.

In the fourteenth century it was impossible for a
cultivated poet to be insular. Chaucer learned his
art and drew much of his material from foreign
literature, ancient and modern. He was especially

attracted by the *Romance of the Rose*, which nourished both his fondness for the dream-vision and his satirical humour; by Boccaccio, who provided the sources for *Troilus and Criseyde* and the *Knight's Tale* (Chaucer apparently did not know the *Decameron*); by Ovid, the supreme story-teller of the Middle Ages and Renaissance; and by Boethius, whose *Consolation of Philosophy* was an abiding supplement to his Catholic faith. Chaucer read and borrowed from a multitude of other authors, major and minor, such as the French poets of his own age, Petrarch, Dante (who might not have recognized the professorial eagle of *The House of Fame*), and Virgil, whose epic was for Chaucer as for his fellows the story of the betrayal of the faithful Dido. In short, he was a poet of cosmopolitan culture who stood as a matter of course in the full stream of the European tradition.

It is a commonplace though always a surprising fact that, in the literary countries generally, the subtleties of poetic technique have been mastered earlier than the simplicities of prose, and one example is the difference between Chaucer's unwieldy prose and his supple verse. He was a sophisticated craftsman in numerous metrical and stanzaic forms of lyrical and narrative poetry. The octosyllabics of the *House of Fame*, the rhyme royal of *Troilus*, and the pentameter couplets of most of the *Canterbury Tales* were all adapted with flexible ease to the varying demands of action, description, and dialogue. Chaucer was apparently the inventor, and one of the great masters, of what was to be later known as the heroic couplet, though the name calls up a clipped antithetical pattern far removed from his; Chaucer's couplets flow and ripple and eddy with the informal artlessness of everyday speech. And his style and diction have—except where a higher key is wanted—a corresponding informality. The reader is seldom made aware that Chaucer was, like other poets, steeped in the 'colours of rhetoric' that medieval scholars loved to formulate. Everyone remembers how the unrhetorical franklin smilingly pricked his own unwonted bubble of inflation:

> *For th'orisonte hath reft the sonne his lyght,—*
> *This is as muche to seye as it was nyght!*

In his colloquial style and movement, and in his combining of ironic suggestion with concrete precision, Chaucer is a very modern writer—although his staple texture is 'prose statement' and cannot very well be analysed in terms of ambiguity, paradox, and other modern shibboleths.

Narrative in verse has gone out of fashion nowadays, but it was—before the advent of the novel—one of the principal genres. Chaucer possessed, in a superlative degree, the gifts required for both the short story and the novel—and we might add the drama, since *Troilus and Criseyde* is largely presented in dramatic scenes and much of the comedy of the *Tales* is dramatic. The story of Troilus, Criseyde, and Diomede had been created and elaborated by a succession of medieval writers, and it was in England the main offshoot of the central romance of Troy. Such a pseudo-classical tale, reflecting the life and manners of the Middle Ages, was not a product of 'medieval *naïveté*'; it was in the tradition of modernizing begun by Ovid, or indeed by Homer himself, and often carried on in our own time. Chaucer's insight into universal human feelings was not dulled by a concern for archaeology. Nor was it distorted by his accepting the conventions of courtly love. Boccaccio's *Filostrato*, though it added the author's personal experience to the traditional story, was only an erotic romance. Chaucer deepened and enriched character and motive and gave the romantic plot new tensions and dimensions. In his poem Troy is at once a scene of authentic everyday living and a besieged city with whose fate that of the lovers is bound up. The widowed Criseyde is a sober gentlewoman who can realistically weigh the attractions of independence and surrender, and in the end she sinks to infidelity, not because she is a wanton, but because her love is of the kind that 'cannot admit Absence'. Pandarus, now her elderly uncle, is a humorous man of the world who is willing to bring Troilus and Criseyde together; yet even he is stricken by the consciousness of having betrayed both his niece and his friend. The rules and motives of courtly love gave Chaucer, not a tissue of artificial emotions, but a naturalism of sophisticated refinement. The growth and power of such love—which, it was recognized, had its ennobling side—he could set forth with the imaginative sympathy of a great artist, and yet, as the moving epilogue makes explicit, with the ultimate judgment of a Christian who recoils from the false and fleeting joys of the world of passion. When Matthew Arnold found Chaucer wanting in 'high seriousness', he must have forgotten the poet's finest completed work.

The reader who neglects *Troilus* and identifies Chaucer with the *Canterbury Tales* misses an essential part of him. In the *Tales*, of course, his

comic vision, already active in *Troilus,* has full
scope. And even the best of the tales are not better
than the descriptions of the dramatis personae in the
General Prologue. After the opening paragraph,
with its delicate and buoyant springtime freshness,
the material is the commonplace world of prose, but
the result is no less obviously poetry. The heterogeneous band of pilgrims are thoroughly representative of the fourteenth-century commonalty (no one
above the rank of a knight would join such a party),
and naturally include a large proportion of ecclesiastical figures, from the ease-loving monk and the
dainty prioress and the poor parson to such rascals
as the pardoner, the friar, and the summoner. And
the motive that brings together the genteel and the
uncouth, the devout and the irresponsible, casts an
ironic light upon all the comedy of the road. The
pilgrimage is a sanctified junket, but for many of the
pilgrims sanctity begins and ends at Canterbury.
Chaucer reports on good, average, and bad with
equal minuteness and gusto; they are all human
beings and all children of Mother Church. One
great stroke of originality was the fluid and dramatic
framework, all the business and talk of the journey—
the astute and masterful generalship of Harry
Bailly, the quarrels of the drunken miller and the
reeve and the friar and the summoner, the candid
disclosures of domestic tribulations and triumphs.
Some of Chaucer's comic characters, like some of
Shakespeare's and Dickens's, are conscious humorists
who dramatize themselves.

Apart from allegory, the tales represent about all
the major and minor medieval genres: romance in
several varieties, including the squire's half-told tale

that attracted Spenser and Milton, and also the mock-heroic piece that Chaucer himself recites until stopped by the host; several fabliaux, those comic bourgeois tales which are broader than they are long, and among which the miller's is a masterpiece of construction and vivid detail; the miracle of the Virgin; the saint's legend; the sermon *exemplum*, in the macabre tale of the pardoner and the tale of that lay preacher, the wife of Bath; the beast-fable, in the tale of the cock and the fox; and so on. Some stories of unmitigated patience and pathos, and two large chunks of edification in prose, were evidently more or less relished by the pilgrims and by the author, who at such times seems less close to us than he usually is.

We may wonder also how a poet who could write the wife's prologue, or the tale of January and May and the other fabliaux, could treat love in the purely romantic vein of the knight's or the franklin's tale. But whereas the modern poet is normally committed to writing with his whole being, the medieval (or Renaissance) poet could enjoy himself, or parts of himself, on quite different planes, without letting his right hand be cramped by what his left hand did. Whether this habit of mind implies a dissociated or a unified sensibility, the masters of the subtle schools of criticism may determine. But we might say that Chaucer's varied instincts, for romantic idealism and bawdy humour, for pathos and satire, are all made possible, and are unified, by a secure religious creed. He can look at his human creations just as God made them.

The serious tales, and the chosen modes of treatment, seldom bring into play the psychological

tensions and ironic complexities of *Troilus*. The
pardoner's soul has sometimes been made the scene
of anguished conflict, but the simple truth would
seem to be that he has to go through his professional
act and also has to be shown up as a scoundrel, and
that Chaucer, like Elizabethan dramatists, puts the
exposure, without worrying about consistency, into
the character's own mouth. If comedy anywhere
rises into tragic irony, it is in the wife's prologue.
She is not a mere female Sweeney. With all her animal
grossness, she has her inward twinges, of a sort:

> *But, Lord Crist! whan that it remembreth me*
> *Upon my yowthe, and on my jolitee,*
> *It tikleth me aboute myn herte roote.*
> *Unto this day it dooth myn herte boote*
> *That I have had my world as in my tyme.*
> *But age, allas! that al wol envenyme,*
> *Hath me biraft my beautee and my pith.*
> *Lat go, farewel! the devel go therwith! . . .*
>
> *Allas! allas! that evere love was synne!*

The wife's self-revelation is both fuller and briefer
than Mrs. Bloom's—and no one would try to elevate
her into an Earth Goddess.

There is really no accounting for Chaucer, for his
compassionate and humorous irony, for the casual
ease and deftness of his poetic art. If he had not
existed, it would not have been necessary to invent
him; we should have accepted his friend the worthy
John Gower as the natural and logical poet of the
later fourteenth century.

Chaucer's satire on ecclesiastical figures and
abuses, lively as it was, did not go beyond what

might come from any loyal son of the church; it was only when the parson rebuked him for swearing that Harry Bailly smelled a Lollard in the wind. But the *Vision of Piers Plowman* (1362–87?) was a work of bitter protest and earnest exhortation. The dream-allegory, the frame of so many medieval poems, is not here put to Chaucer's fanciful and decorative uses, but is, in its homespun way, Dantesque. Nor does the clerical William Langland (whether he was one man or several) survey the field full of folk with the eager, objective curiosity of Chaucer at the Tabard Inn or on the Canterbury road. Langland is a seeker of Christ and salvation, a crusader and prophet, whose vision of Truth and Love, of what a Christian England might be, rises out of his harsh recognition of sin among high and low, secular and religious. He is an early Bunyan, intent on describing what he sees, the world of Vanity Fair, and on persuading his readers to gain a better world, here and hereafter. To quote Christopher Dawson (*Religion and the Rise of Western Culture*):

'Langland's poem is the last and in some respects the most uncompromising expression of the medieval ideal of the unity of religion and culture. He realized more clearly than the poets and more intensely than the philosophers that religion was not a particular way of life but the way of all life, and that the divine love which is "the leader of the Lord's folk of heaven" is also the law of life upon earth.'

The *Vision* is a work of art, in design and in details, and it contains passages of a kind quite beyond

Chaucer's reach; yet it remains, for most of us, a sombre signpost rather than a poetic possession. That is partly our fault; but it is partly because Langland's imaginative, structural, and stylistic powers are not often enough fused to make poetry equal to his theme.

While Langland and Chaucer may stand as exemplars, respectively, of native tradition and foreign influence, they may also be described—if we adjust our sights—as both English and both European. The same double label must be attached to the large body of romances, ballads, and religious lyrics. Arthurian romance, 'the matter of Britain', was one of the three medieval divisions of European fiction. Chaucer, whose tales in general were so typical of medieval taste, used Arthurian romance only once, and then incidentally, in his version of the widespread story of 'the loathly lady'. The cruder romances we take on trust, through *Sir Thopas*, but the early tales of such English heroes as Guy of Warwick and Bevis of Hampton remained popular for centuries among the unsophisticated. The sophisticated romance, the diversion of hall and bower rather than ale-house, has its best representatives in Chaucer's *Knight's Tale* and in *Gawain and the Green Knight*. The latter is by far the finest English piece of Arthurian romance. It rises above the type in its skilful plot and dialogue and general artistic power, in its vivid hunting scenes and its pictures of nature both benign and wintry, and in its special mixture of chivalric idealism and innocuous diablerie. But for us the other romances of Arthur's knights and ladies live in the prose of Malory and some of the modern poems based on him, and we

cannot linger with a shelf of verse that enjoys only
the life-in-death of scholarly regard.

To turn to what really lives, there is the body of
lyrical poetry, secular and religious, and the great
fact about most of these poems is that they were
lyrics, that they were sung and composed for singing. We must neglect miscellaneous secular lyrics,
such as the early and famous *Alison*, for the more
distinctive English and Scottish ballads, which came
into being especially in the fifteenth century, though
there were some earlier and many later ones. A
popular ballad may be roughly defined as a short
poem that tells or implies a story, commonly of one
episode, and that was sung or recited. The English
and Scottish ballads followed the kind of conventions
usually found in popular poetry. The familiar and
largely typical *Sir Patrick Spens* illustrates the so-
called ballad metre; there were, however, other
metrical patterns, and many ballads had a refrain.
The poem illustrates also the chief characteristics of
the ballad manner: impersonal and dramatic objectivity; the abrupt alternation of narrative and speech;
parallelism of structure, often with incremental
repetition; the use of stock phrases and epithets; a
stark simplicity of both imagination and style,
effective alike for concrete realism and romantic
glamour, tragic passion and tragic action, for
humour and a pathos rarely softened by sentimentality. But the story of *Sir Patrick Spens* is not
typical of ballad themes. A very large proportion
deal with innocent or illicit love, and the ending is
perhaps more commonly fatal than happy. The
situations may be those of our newspaper scandals
and crimes, but, thanks to style, setting, and

atmosphere, vice loses half its evil by losing all its grossness—though discovery may lead to brutal punishment. At least one lover is likely to be of gentle birth and both may be; and sometimes a mortal is loved by a fay. Other ballads, like the grim *Edward*, tell of personal enmities or family feuds. Then there are the martial and heroic ballads that have to do with Border warfare, legitimate or illegitimate. We may not care to remember that some of the Border heroes were the gangsters of their day, but the ballads celebrate individual courage and prowess like that of Johnie Armstrong:

> *Saying, Fight on, my merry men all,*
> *And see that none of you be taine;*
> *For I will stand by and bleed but awhile,*
> *And then will I come and fight againe.*

Beyond other ballad heroes, Robin Hood, the great-hearted friend of the poor, the foe of tyrannous nobles, sheriffs, and oppressive authority, had all the elements of popular appeal; and the doings of him and his men in the merry greenwood formed a miniature epic of high-spirited adventure, boisterous comedy, and proletarian sympathy.

The ballads are the mirror of the English and Scottish heroic age, Homeric lays that no Homer came to elevate and unify. They constitute a body of poetry that is at once realistic and idealized, savage and sophisticated. Though the outlaw Robin Hood felt his religious obligations, the ballads in general, apart from those on religious themes, contain few conspicuous signs of having been composed in a Christian land. Heaven and hell,

God and Mary and the Saviour, may be appealed
to in moments of stress, and the church exists,
mainly as a place for burial, but the prevailing moral
code is more barbaric than Christian. The sword is
ready to every man's hand and violence and death
are an everyday affair. Love, whether adulterous or
simply lacking the marriage bond, is for lovers its
own justification; and though by husbands and
brothers it may be seen as a crime against family
honour, it is not held up as a sin.

At the other end of the spectrum is the world of
simple and pure devotion reflected in the religious
lyrics. Heaven and Christ and His Mother lose none
of their bright beauty in being brought very close
to earth and man. Many lyrics are of course celebrations of Christmas and show all the medieval
instinct for the human elements of the Nativity.
Two of the most familiar lyrics illustrate the range of
treatment. There is the *naïveté* of adoration so
abundantly poured out before the Virgin:

> *I sing of a maiden*
> *   That is makeles;*
> *King of all kings*
> *   To her son she ches. . . .*
>
> *Mother and maiden*
> *   Was never none but she;*
> *Well may such a lady*
> *   Goddes mother be.*

In the more complex and dramatic *Quia amore
langueo*, Christ's love for the soul of man is rendered
in terms of human relations and secular love poetry,
and these contrasts involve the further contrasts

between his divine love and power and his human suffering:

> *My fair love and my spouse bright!*
> *I saved her from beating, and she hath me bet;*
> *I clothed her in grace and heavenly light;*
> *This bloody shirt she hath on me set. . . .*

This is the kind of paradox that in a later age we call baroque (and we think of George Herbert when Christ says, 'Fair love, let us go dine'). Popular ballads are still composed in modern times, but the medieval religious lyrics are inimitable survivals of a long-vanished world. In them, as in primitive paintings or the best of the mystery plays, the divine story is concrete and natural, human and tender, and transparent purity of style is born of reverent purity of emotion.

Though medieval strains of thought and feeling were to flow on into the seventeenth century, the last full flowering of medievalism was in the Scottish Chaucerians. The best of them, Robert Henryson (*c.* 1425–*c.* 1506) and William Dunbar (*c.* 1460–*c.* 1520), make real claims upon us; so too does Gavin Douglas's translation of the *Aeneid* (1513; printed 1553). They have suffered, however, as even Burns has, because of the language that is part of their strength; glossaries are non-conductors of vitality and flavour. Both Henryson and Dunbar bring artistic and emotional originality and force to old traditions. Henryson's *Robene and Makyne*, which blends the charming artifice of the *pastourelle* with the homely realities of Scottish life and character, has a more authentic ring than its English counterpart, *The Nut-Brown Maid*, which is also charming but rather too smooth and elegant. Henryson's Aesopic fables, notably the Horatian *Tale of the Uplandish Mouse and the Burgess Mouse*, show the lively and ironical mixture of human and animal worlds that we know best from Chaucer. But it was in the tragic irony of his sequel to Chaucer, *The Testament of Cresseid*, that Henryson reached his highest level. No one can forget the conclusion, the picture of the leprous Cresseid, a beggar at the town's end, receiving lavish alms from Troilus as he rides by and is stirred by her disfigured face to a sudden vision of his old love. Here the poet's compassionate imagination transcends his moral judgment.

The courtier Dunbar is less homely than Henryson, and more diversified, more fantastic, and—as in the piece on the two married women and the widow— more scurrilous. The *Ballad of Kind Kittok*, whether it is Dunbar's or not, displays that medieval humour which familarly embraces heaven as well as earth. In *The Dance of the Seven Deadly Sins* the ancient religious theme is quickly submerged in earthly and earthy realism. Above all, there is the *Lament for the Makers*, the great British parallel to Villon's *Ballade of Old-Time Ladies*. The names of Dunbar's Scottish poets are mostly as unfamiliar as FitzGerald's Jamshyd and Bahram, but the brief allusions call up full-blooded men, and the names themselves are poetry. Then the tolling bell of the refrain, *Timor mortis conturbat me*, combines suggestions of universal destiny and universal ritual with a personal shudder.

John Skelton (*c.* 1460–1529) brings us through the

first quarter of the sixteenth century, but in spirit and manner he belongs, with all his original force, rather to the Middle Ages than to the Renaissance. He was an almost exact contemporary of Dunbar, and a world away from his younger English contemporary, Sir Thomas Wyatt. He was a transitional mixture, not so much of the old and the new as of the old and himself. He celebrated the stock trinity, Chaucer, Gower, and Lydgate, but, though many writers lumped them together or put Lydgate first, Skelton's warmest praise was given to Chaucer. While he largely broke away from courtly stereotypes and aureate language, his subjects and attitudes and tone were more or less medieval. His favourite metre, the tumbling, breathless short line that is identified with him, has been traced to medieval Latin verse and prose. His uncritical literary learning, poured out in appropriate or inappropriate places, was that of a late medieval Latinist, not of a new humanist and Grecian. Skelton's leaping allusiveness and rhetorical 'amplification' cannot perhaps be called peculiarly medieval, but at least bear small relation to Italianate ideals; the reader never knows what is coming next. At times we are reminded of that great man of prose, Rabelais, who combined humanism with high jinks. Skelton's own descriptions of his writing are the best:

> For though my rhyme be ragged,
> Tattered and jagged,
> Rudely rain-beaten,
> Rusty and moth-eaten,
> If ye take well therewith,
> It hath in it some pith.

One feels that Skelton, for all his literary prestige and court connexions, was as artist an isolated figure, and that isolation nourished his eccentricity. It is of course his eccentricity, his individual 'pith' and energetic directness, and his 'sprung rhythm', that have in our day brought about a Skeltonic revival.

As a priest and devoted son of the Church, Skelton was impelled to explosive attacks on ecclesiastical corruption and Cardinal Wolsey, and corruption at court as well. In manner he stands midway between Langland and the Protestant satirists up through Spenser and Milton. He does not as a rule use the dream-allegory, and he lacks the detached dramatic irony of Chaucer; he relies rather on concrete recital and invective. He is a man of outraged conscience who lays about him with a flail. But much of his satire has paid the usual penalty of minute topicality, and modern readers turn rather to *Philip Sparrow* and *The Tunning of Elinor Rumming*. These two pieces illustrate the range of the poet's sensibility and manner. In his account of Jane Scrope's grief for the death of her pet sparrow he can fuse playful tenderness with liturgical burlesque of the Goliardic kind; and he can, with a racy toughness still permitted to clerics, give an unrivalled genre picture of female topers gathering for a boozing party. Yet the *Tunning* is all in one key, the characters are all seen from the outside; and we may think of how much richer the subject would have been in the hands of Chaucer or Dunbar.

In most respects great medieval poetry has the qualities that make great poetry in any period and language. But if we could imagine its being read by someone whose knowledge had been limited to the poetry of our century, such a reader would be struck by some large differences. One might be the amount of freedom possessed by the modern as contrasted with the medieval poet. While modern poetry has its own idiom, the assumption is that every poem is an independent rendering of an individual experience, and that the theme and mood will dictate the right form and style. The medieval poet—and poets long after the Middle Ages—recognized various established genres, which had their special conventions of form and manner. But we should not assume that the advantage is all on the side of modern freedom; acceptance of the genres never fettered the originality of a good poet, but was rather a positive aid to him and his readers.

Perhaps the chief surprise for our imaginary reader would be only a large extension of the particular contrast just mentioned: that is, the general absence of the subjective and introspective and the predominance of the objective and impersonal. A high proportion of recent poetry records the mental states of poets who feel at odds with the society and the world in which they find themselves; a high proportion of medieval poems, long and short, are narratives, and many of the stories are the common property of many nations. Of course in telling stories a poet like Chaucer reveals his attitude—or attitudes—towards life, but that is not his aim; he submerges himself in his material, and his material comes from outside. Not regarding himself as an articulate victim of an abhorrent civilization, he responds with zest to the widest variety of tales and characters. Even Langland, who does abhor what he sees in the world, remains in general the impersonal voice of righteousness. And those anonymous lyrics and carols that might be called personal are not expressions of merely private feelings.

Then our twentieth-century reader, accustomed to poetry that is acutely sensitive to the metaphysical, psychological, political, and economic problems of our world, would find most of the large body of medieval narrative 'romantic' and remote from the life and problems of its age. As a general precaution we may remember that the realities of the medieval world tend to become romantic for later ages—and also that the realities of our mechanized world, from the toaster to television, would for the medieval man be wildly romantic. But in medieval poetry questions of metaphysical or religious belief hardly ever come up (though Troilus feels caught in the toils of necessity) because all people in their various ways hold the same creed. Romances and ballads, while they have some basis in feudalism and chivalry, are more or less stylized in plot and substance as well as in diction; they do not answer many of the questions about feudalism, or about love and marriage and home life, that interest the modern historian. On these topics we may of course learn much from Chaucer and others, though not as a rule from their full-dress romances. Yet the medieval poet has a strong instinct for the realistic and concrete, even in stories of impossible virtue and impossible ordeals, or in stories of the supernatural. A story is a story, whether English or Oriental, realistic or romantic.

Chaucer has been an available if inimitable model

from the fifteenth century up to the very un-Chaucerian Imagists and Mr. Masefield, but his influence in the modern centuries has generally been too impalpable for demonstration. The recurrent influence of the ballads is much more obvious. They have always been there—though not always in print and not always esteemed—as an example and source of elemental strength and economy as well as a mirror of a world of passion and action. We recall how Sir Philip Sidney, the first English classicist, revealed the gap between his instinctive and his acquired taste:

'Certainly, I must confess my own barbarous-ness, I never heard the old song of Percy and Douglas that I found not my heart moved more than with a trumpet; and yet is it sung but by some blind crowder, with no rougher voice than rude style; which, being so evil apparelled in the dust and cobwebs of that uncivil age, what would it work, trimmed in the gorgeous eloquence of Pindar?'

And in the early eighteenth century Addison felt the need of justifying admiration for the ballads by citing classical parallels. Bishop Percy's collection, though mixed with later poetry and though subjected to a smoothing editorial hand, did much to establish the ballads in their own right. But the salutary influence of the ballads on romantic poetry must wait for a later chapter. The essence of medievalism, in ballads or carols, in Chaucer or Langland, could not be revived.

CHAPTER II

THE RENAISSANCE

ALTHOUGH Sir Thomas Wyatt (1503?–42) began his diplomatic career, and presumably his writing of poetry, before the death of Skelton, he belonged to a new world, the world of the Italian Renaissance. He was well acquainted with Italy, France, and Spain. The first considerable collection of his poems was published, with those of Henry Howard, Earl of Surrey (1517?–47) and others, in *Songs and Sonnets,* commonly known as *Tottel's Miscellany* (1557), so that he has often been treated rather as a harbinger of the Elizabethan age than as a notable poet in his own right. But, without slighting the historical importance of Wyatt's introduction of the sonnet (and the *ottava rima, terza rima,* the epigram, and semi-classical satire), modern critics have come to recognize the power and beauty of his lyrics or 'ballets'. In these he was not self-consciously domesticating an exotic genre but was carrying on, with distinctive individuality, the native lyrical modes of the fifteenth and early sixteenth centuries. For instance, as Mr. Tillyard points out, the simplicity of the medieval carol, 'I sing of a maiden' (of which some lines were quoted in the first chapter), reappears in Wyatt's 'What should I say?':

> *I promised you,*
> *And you promised me,*
> *To be as true*
> *As I would be.*

Whatever the amorous joys and pains of Wyatt the full-blooded man, no doubt there is often as much artifice in his lyrics as in his sonnets, but in the many good ones artifice is handled with assured ease; and the poet-lutanist is tireless in metrical experimentation. Moreover, at his best he is not laboriously plaintive and abject before a disdainful mistress; rather, as in 'Forget not yet the tried intent', he pleads or chides with dignity as well as passion. We are reminded sometimes, if distantly, of Donne: along with intensity, Wyatt has touches of outward and inward drama and of self-analysis, and his staple language is plain, 'unpoetical', often monosyllabic English. But while Donne's love-poems are seldom songs, Wyatt works his many variations within the lyrical frame and rhythm. One triumph is the delicately hovering, wondering movement, and the dramatic mixture of personal involvement and detachment, in

> *They flee from me that sometime did me seek,*
> *With naked foot stalking in my chamber . . .*
>
> *It was no dream; I lay broad waking.*
> *But all is turned thorough my gentleness*
> *Into a strange fashion of forsaking. . . .*

Except in his satires, Wyatt pays little attention to the external world; the stage of his amatory poems is his own heart. Surrey—one of whose best pieces is the tribute to his master, 'W. resteth here, that quick could never rest'—shows a wider range of interest (though not of form), and, in poems of love as well as others, he is aware of humanity and the

natural world. A lonely woman thinks thus envi-
ously of happy pairs of lovers:

> *I stand the bitter night*
> *In my window, where I may see*
> *Before the winds how the clouds flee.*
> *Lo! what a mariner love hath made me!*

But, though Surrey reveals facets of his aristocratic
and forceful personality, his smooth fluency rarely
achieves the poignant concentration and rhythm of
the lines just cited, or of Wyatt. We are not irresist-
ibly drawn to read him; instead we pay our formal
respects to the moulder of the sonnet and the
inventor of blank verse—and perhaps heave a sigh
over his propagation of 'poulter's measure'.

From *Tottel's Miscellany* onward, individual poets
emerge more distinctly, though even these courtly
makers are mostly amateurs (and though even
seventeenth-century manuscript collections include
many poems of doubtful authorship). When we
survey the great body of Tudor and later song, the
most remarkable fact is the wide distribution of the
lyrical gift. From Henry VIII (who shared with
Wyatt an attachment to the Muse as well as to Anne
Boleyn), and courtiers who otherwise seem hard-
headed worldlings, down to rakehelly Elizabethan
journalists, almost anyone can write beautiful and
moving songs on love and youth and age and death.
At one pole is that early and piercing cry of ballad-
like simplicity:

> *Western wind, when will thou blow,*
> *The small rain down can rain?*
> *Christ, if my love were in my arms*
> *And I in my bed again!*

At the opposite pole is such a later, longer, and lighter product of anonymity as the courtly and very popular broadside ballad of 'the Lady Greensleeves'. But even the work of the great Elizabethan lyrists whom we know retains a high degree of impersonality. Whereas a lyric of Wordsworth or Shelley instantly proclaims its author, it would be a bold critic who could, on internal evidence, sort out the lyrics of Lyly (or those that pass as his), Peele, Greene, Lodge, Nashe, Breton, and others, including Shakespeare. One reason for such impersonality was that the lyrists were not moved by the desire for 'self-expression' or radical novelty, but were working within a set of more or less artificial conventions, literary and musical. Such conventions—if we read right through the song-books, even Campion's— may become thinly monotonous, since the songs were written to be heard, and not heard all at once. But a multitude of songs are satisfying as poetry without the music.

One convention, which developed as the century advanced, was Italianate and classical pastoralism, a convention that came to full flower in the most charming of Elizabethan anthologies, *England's Helicon* (1600). In the idyllic Arcadia of pastoral song, it is always the merry month of May, and the pangs of Petrarchan lovers rarely strike Phyllida and Corydon. Samela combines the bright beauties of all the goddesses. Rosalind, in whose bosom Love sucks like a bee, is—to soar from pastoral sweets to the celestial world—

> *Like to the clear in highest sphere,*
> *Where all empyreal glory shines.*

If we needed proof of the strength of the convention, we might remember that it drew from the fiery spirit of Marlowe what was to be the most famous of all pastoral lyrics, 'Come live with me and be my love'. But, although so many men contributed to the treasury of song, Shakespeare reigns here as elsewhere; no other poet displayed such variety of theme and tone on such a high level of felicity. Many of his lyrics—'Who is Silvia?' 'It was a lover and his lass', 'O mistress mine, where are you roaming?' 'When daffodils begin to peer'—are conventional dallyings with the innocence of love, yet literary pastoralism can extend to robust realism—Dick the shepherd blowing his nail and red-nosed Marian and greasy Joan. There is moralizing on life that ranges from 'Under the greenwood tree' and 'When that I was and a little tiny boy' to 'Fear no more the heat o' the sun'. And there is the iridescent magic, 'of the water, watery', of 'Full fathom five thy father lies'. Shakespeare's songs in general have the simple texture and tunefulness, the air of easy spontaneity, that belong to popular tradition.

But Tudor lyricism, though it created a paradise of amatory and idyllic make-believe, was not entirely divorced from life (and the pastoral ideal was in part a rejection of the ways of the world). As Shakespeare's graver notes remind us, the hazards of fortune and ambition and death were dark realities in an age of violence, feud, and capricious royal favour. And classical humanism furnished materials and models, such as Horace and Martial, for ethical reflection that was not merely Polonian. So we have, from courtiers like Wyatt and Surrey

and Bacon, and more obscure observers of mutability, distrust of the vainglorious world and praise
of the mean and sure estate. 'My mind to me a
kingdom is', declared Sir Edward Dyer. Chidiock
Tichborne, executed in 1586 for his share in the
Babington plot, gives his meditations a refrain—
'And now I live, and now my life is done'—that
sounds like thuds of earth into his grave. A generation later Sir Walter Ralegh (1552?–1618), rewriting
some earlier lines of his own just before his execution,
provides a personal and religious parallel to the great
apostrophe to Death in the *History:*

> *Even such is Time, which takes in trust*
> *Our youth, our joys, and all we have,*
> *And pays us but with age and dust. . . .*

Indeed much of Ralegh's verse, so strongly individual
in substance and manner that it cannot be linked
with any school or fashion, is a disenchanted denial
of both the Arcadian dream and the mundane ends
that he himself pursued. To 'Come live with me and
be my love' he replies with a sober recognition of the
fading of youth and love and pleasure. In other
poems, wanton desire is the grave of reason; life is a
'play of passion', a 'short comedy' except in its final
curtain. With explosive directness Ralegh gives the
lie to the court and the world, to the whole fabric
of corruption that society maintains. And, with a
fervour that engenders some bizarre images, the
passionate man would take his scallop shell of quiet,
his staff of faith to walk upon, for his pilgrimage
toward 'heaven's bribeless hall'.

Along with the deceits and illusions of the stage-
play world there was the stark fact of death, which

quickened or darkened even celebrations of young love, and which had both a special horror and an everyday familiarity in an age of recurrent plagues. The universal theme could stir the exuberantly slangy pamphleteer, Thomas Nashe, to a recital of the great commonplaces, from which rises one stanza of bare simplicity and rich suggestion:

> Beauty is but a flower
> Which wrinkles will devour;
> Brightness falls from the air,
> Queens have died young and fair,
> Dust hath closed Helen's eye.
> I am sick, I must die.
>   Lord, have mercy on us!

First comes the theme of a thousand Renaissance versions of 'Carpe diem'; then an image at once concrete and meteorological,[1] abstract and magical, 'Brightness falls from the air'; then the tradition of 'Ubi sunt . . . ?' and the dance of Death, who laid low the queens of the earth, even the most lovely and glamorous woman of pagan myth; and then a Christian prayer.

In the sixteenth century the word 'sonnet' did not have its modern precise meaning but was loosely equivalent to 'song'. Concerning the structure of the sonnet proper a few bald facts may be noted. Wyatt normally followed the Petrarchan octave (abbaabba), though a couple of times he deserted the Italian form to use new rhymes in the second quatrain. In the sestet he did not follow Petrarch;

---

[1] That is, if Nashe did not write *hayre* (hair) instead of *ayre* (*Works*, ed. McKerrow, iv, 440). We may prefer magic to logic.

in almost all of his more than thirty sonnets the sestet broke naturally into a quatrain and a couplet. With such models before him, and with a consciousness of the paucity of rhymes in English, Surrey developed and regularized the 'English' sonnet of three quatrains, each with its own rhymes, and a couplet (*ababcdcdefefgg*). The Elizabethan sonneteers commonly adopted this pattern or variations of it; Milton and later poets generally preferred the Italian form. The difference involved more than mere mechanics. Whereas the Italian sonnet has two more or less distinct sections, in an English sonnet the thought and images tend to flow into the triple-quatrain division, and the final couplet is likely to become an epigrammatic or gnomic conclusion.

The posthumous and unauthorized publication of Sir Philip Sidney's *Astrophel and Stella* in 1591 started the vogue of sonneteering that drew elaborate sequences from Daniel, Lodge, Drayton, Spenser, Shakespeare, and many smaller poets. Petrarch— 'poor Petrarch's long-deceased woes', in Sidney's phrase—had now been largely superseded by later French and Italian models, but the convention was essentially unchanged; and, although we have of late been taught more respect for formal artifice, few of us can respond to the protracted chills and fevers, self-abasements and adorations, of Petrarchan love, and to the fanciful and extravagant conceits that make up the common texture of such verse. The good poets have of course their successes. Drayton's two strains of Elizabethan idealism and anti-romantic revulsion are blended in his late and famous 'Since there's no help, come let us kiss and part'; the forthright dramatic directness of the first quatrains gives way to a semi-dramatic grouping of allegorical abstractions which heighten the seriousness and suspense of the lover's wavering and surrender. But even Shakespeare can weary us, or at least arouse less wholehearted satisfaction than wonder at his resources of ingenuity. We may look at his sequence and Sidney's.

While the question of 'sincerity'—in the sense of actual as distinguished from imaginative experience —is irrelevant here as elsewhere, we have Sidney's word (in his *Apology for Poetry*) for the genuineness of his passion; its object was evidently Lady Rich. Whatever our guess about Shakespeare, we know nothing. At any rate we have the poems, and we may glance first at the matter of technique. Earlier Tudor poets had to face the special prosodic problems created by post-Chaucerian changes in the language and not altogether solved by fifteenth-century writers—the definition of the pentameter line in terms of the number of stresses or the number of syllables, the nature and extent of variations from the norm, the harmonizing of the metrical pattern with the pattern of thought. In the third quarter of the century perhaps the chief danger was a wooden regularity. But in *Astrophel and Stella*— and Spenser's *Shepherd's Calendar*—poetry reached a maturity from which there was to be no relapse. Both poets were conscious students of technique, and Sidney must have profited from his sometimes fine experiments in quantitative metre. Among the virtues of his sonnets is the capacity for flexible variation and progressive movement that marks assured control. In more than technical ways the

opening sonnet, a declaration of independence, is as
fine an example as any of a poet's seeking and finding
freedom for personal utterance within a convention
that rather sustains than hampers him. The combination of simple language and rhetorical artifice at
once reveals and dignifies personal feeling, and the
final couplet is a direct and dramatic climax:

> *Biting my truant pen, beating myself for spite,*
> *'Fool', said my Muse to me, 'look in thy heart and*
>   *write.'*

Apart from technique, what gives dramatic reality to
the whole sequence is the moral and religious conflict
it embodies. A knight of chivalry, a Platonist, and
a Christian loves the wife of another, and he knows,
like a medieval courtly lover, that his love is
ennobling, that it engages his deepest and highest
emotions. Yet if it is bound up with virtue and
honour, it is also a betrayal of both: 'Desire still
cries, "Give me some food."' In the end—if a
separate sonnet can be related to the sequence—the
Christian ideal conquers, at least dramatically, and
the renunciation takes us back to the conclusion
of Chaucer's *Troilus*:

> *Leave me, O love, which reacheth but to dust;*
> *And thou, my mind, aspire to higher things;*
> *Grow rich in that which never taketh rust,*
> *Whatever fades but fading pleasure brings. . . .*

Shakespeare's sonnets, published in 1609 when the
vogue had long subsided, were in the main written,
it may be presumed, in the fifteen-nineties; their
rhetorical amplitude of line and rhythm seems to

link them with the narrative poems and earlier plays. Themes, images, and texture range from thin artifice to 'classical' grandiloquence or 'metaphysical' density, but language, however poignant, remains predominantly simple. Happily we cannot go into the manifold problems that have raised around the sonnets an almost impenetrable barricade of commentary. Even the arrangement is beset with puzzles; not all of the first 126 sonnets seem to be addressed to one young man, and CXXVII-CLII, though apparently addressed to the Dark Lady, do not form a consecutive series. While the central situation is unusual, much of Shakespeare's analysis of love may be applied to man and woman as well as man and man. His idealistic view of love appears in the sonnets to the young man; the sinister Dark Lady inspires hostile and racking thoughts of 'Th' expense of spirit in a waste of shame'. Shakespeare can be deeply moved by a religious consciousness of sin, though for the most part his joys and griefs are those of the natural man. The poet-lover has enemies without and within—disloyalty, jealousy, lust, hate—but the ever-present enemy of youth and love and hope and happiness is remorseless Time. Although 'Full many a glorious morning' gilds meadows and streams with heavenly alchemy, the sun of his life is 'but one hour mine'. He can at moments utter a defiance—

Love's not Time's fool, though rosy lips and cheeks
Within his bending sickle's compass come—

yet our dominant impression is not of the lark that sings hymns at heaven's gate but of an autumnal mood of resignation—'Bare ruin'd choirs where late the sweet birds sang'.

The chief strains of lyrical poetry, the pastoral amorousness of youth and the ethical sobriety of age, were writ large, so to speak, in the Ovidian narrative and the long reflective poem. The best examples of Ovidian narrative are of course Marlowe's *Hero and Leander* (1593?) and Shakespeare's *Venus and Adonis* (1593). This kind of writing, like so many other kinds, carried on a European fashion. The luscious pictorial elaboration of such poems, which went beyond the highly pictorial Ovid, was a literary parallel to much Renaissance painting. It exemplified to the full the aesthetic doctrine crystallized in the phrase *ut pictura poesis*, the doctrine that painting is silent poetry and poetry a speaking picture. Classical mythology was ransacked not only for the main stories but for allusions, images, and conceits suggestive of ideal beauty in nature, art, and the human body. We can measure Italianate influence by comparing Marlowe and Shakespeare with mythological descriptions in Chaucer.

Moreover, while medieval poets had been able to find in Ovid the ideals of courtly love, Renaissance Ovidians commonly glorified the fleshliness of neo-pagan eroticism—though English poets seldom did so without a consciousness of orthodox morality. Marlowe's Leander is at times an innocent and worshipful lover, at times a libertine philosopher arguing against conventional restraints, and Hero is both a Juliet and a coquette; and while the poet celebrates youthful raptures with full sympathy, he is also aware of love's cruelty. *Venus and Adonis* (which reverses the situation of the Petrarchan lover

and mistress) perhaps has, on its lower level, more
unity of tone, though Adonis, who seems less chaste
than frigid, can address to the sweating goddess a
little sermon on love and lust. To most readers the
heady ardour and glow of Marlowe's theme and texture are much more attractive than the cool detachment and skilfully contrived rhetoric of Shakespeare; what stands out from the artificial tapestry is
an occasional bit of Warwickshire like the dew-
bedabbled hare.

The Ovidian genre had its variations and exceptions (indeed some scholars see in *Venus and Adonis*
a philosophical treatment of the problem of evil, or
of love). In *Lucrece* (1954) the theme is again lust
and chastity and death, and there is much description and declamation, but whereas *Venus and Adonis*
has affinities with the sonnets, *Lucrece* is akin to
the earlier tragedies and to Senecan drama. Another
kind of exception was Drayton's *Endymion and
Phoebe* (1595), which anticipated Keats's poem in its
'Platonic' fable of the identity of earthly reality
with the heavenly ideal. Such a theme may serve
to remind us of the large debt of Renaissance
poets to the dictionaries of mythology, which were
widely used not merely as collections of myths but
as treasuries of allegorical and symbolic interpretation. These books yielded images and symbols
to such poets as Spenser and especially Chapman
and Jonson. The name of Chapman calls up still
other exceptions to Ovidian eroticism, and that
fashion was indeed condemned by this earnestly
Platonic, Stoic, and Christian poet in the course of
his first work, the difficult *Shadow of Night* (1594).
Chapman adapted the genre to his own purposes in

Ovid's Banquet of Sense, an abstruse analysis of sensory experience in terms of Neoplatonic idealism, and in his elaborate continuation of Marlowe's *Hero and Leander*; this unfinished tale was made over in accordance with Chapman's sober ethical creed, and his closely packed, 'metaphysical' style is equally remote from Marlowe's swift, bright stream of 'classical' rhetoric.

Chapman brings us to the reflective or philosophical poem. This kind of writing was only the most direct manifestation of the established view of the serious poet's function. Poets and critics held with fervour the didactic conception of poetry that had come down from the ancients, the belief in the efficacy of delightful teaching, in the close relation between good letters and virtuous action, in the inspirational power of heroic examples and moral precepts. If we moderns regard such open and palpable didacticism as naïve, we may remember that it had the sanction of many centuries and many great poets and that it was still to animate poets so different as Milton and Pope.

The reflective poem had been nobly inaugurated by a man of action, Thomas Sackville, who was to hold a high place in Elizabeth's councils. His *Induction* to his *Complaint of Henry Duke of Buckingham* (1563) is the only real poem in *The Mirror for Magistrates*, the patriotic, popular, and repeatedly enlarged successor to Lydgate's *Fall of Princes* and Boccaccio's *De Casibus*. The *Induction* is half medieval in its dream-allegory (and Chaucerian language), though the scene is bleak winter and the visionary guide is Sorrow. A Virgilian and Senecan hell discloses such classical abstractions as Dread, Sleep, Old Age, and

Death, but these are described in the medieval emblematic manner (which reappears in Spenser's allegorical pageants). While we might not expect poetry from the co-author of *Gorboduc*, the *Induction* is a massive and moving contemplation of mutability; Sackville feels the great commonplaces of the theme.

In the decades on each side of 1600, four philosophical poets fall into a group—the young lawyer, John (later Sir John) Davies, Samuel Daniel, George Chapman, and Fulke Greville, Lord Brooke, the statesman and 'friend to Sir Philip Sidney'. As thinkers and poets, all have their distinct individuality, but all write within the frame of Christian humanism. That creed, a fusion of the natural wisdom of classical antiquity with the supernatural faith of Christianity, was much less rigorously philosophical, and much more ethical and practical, than the Thomistic synthesis, but it was a later phase of the same central tradition, and it embraced many great names from Erasmus to Hooker, from Spenser to Milton. The keystone is reason, in its fullest sense. Reason and hierarchical order are the law of God and his creation, of society, and of the faculties of the soul. Every creature and thing has an appointed place and function. Man's divine endowment of right reason, though impaired by his fall, is still a sound guide, up to the point where the truths of revelation are needed. In Hooker's words, 'The general and perpetual voice of men is as the sentence of God himself. For that which all men have at all times learned, Nature herself must needs have taught; and God being the author of Nature, her voice is but his instrument.' This metaphysical, social, and ethical structure, resting on belief in a rational God and the rational dignity of man, is inherently optimistic, yet optimism is strongly tempered by a religious and realistic consciousness of man's sinful frailty and rebellious will. In the sixteenth and earlier seventeenth centuries the Christian-humanist synthesis was actively or passively accepted by nearly all writers; but it was pressed hard from one side by the growing numbers of the irrationally religious, from the other by the growing number of the irreligiously rationalistic.

Our four poets are aware of the dangers that threaten their cultural and religious heritage, though they differ in focus and emphasis. In Davies's *Orchestra* (1596), Penelope's chief wooer is the mouthpiece for a graceful interpretation of dancing as a symbol of cosmic Love and an ordered universe; *Nosce Teipsum* (1599) is an earnest exposition of the deceitfulness of human knowledge and of the nature and immortality of the soul. Daniel's *Musophilus* (1599), a debate between a lover of poetry and a philistine worldling, is likewise a prose essay in verse, but the poet's humanistic faith kindles some fire. It is

> *blessed letters, that combine in one*
> *All ages past, and make one live with all.*

And the same faith inspires a vision of the future, of an English literature arising in America:

> *What worlds in th' yet unformëd occident*
> *May come refined with th' accents that are ours?*
> *Or who can tell for what great work in hand*
> *The greatness of our style is now ordained?*

In his weighty epistles to the Countesses of Cumberland and Bedford (and the lyrical *Ulysses and the*

Siren), Daniel's themes are more ethical than literary. He exalts the man of 'resolvĕd powers' who, while pitying the perplexed state 'Of troublous and distressed mortality', dwells in secure wisdom above the turmoil of passion and strife.

The verse of Davies and Daniel has a plain, smooth clarity of statement that may be called neo-classical, and that generally maintains a poetic level through the urgency with which the writers feel the saving doctrines of their creed. Similar ideas, with variations, fortify Chapman and Greville—witness Chapman's *Tears of Peace* and Greville's *Treatie of Humane Learning*—but these two poets have more complex and penetrating minds, a more troubled sense of discord and evil to be overcome. And their verse has a tough—in Chapman's case a darkly figurative—density of thought and phrasing; they struggle to realize and communicate their insights into the disastrous contradictions of man's nature. Yet all four poets face the same problems. Says Davies:

> *I know my life's a pain and but a span,*
> *I know my sense is mocked with everything;*
> *And to conclude, I know myself a man,*
> *Which is a proud and yet a wretched thing.*

Greville, in a chorus of *Mustapha*, makes the antitheses more acute and arresting:

> *Oh wearisome condition of humanity!*
> *Born under one law, to another bound:*
> *Vainly begot, and yet forbidden vanity;*
> *Created sick, commanded to be sound:*
> *What meaneth Nature by these diverse laws?*
> *Passion and Reason self-division cause.*

Chapman, abhorring both worldly ignorance and learned pedantry, can plead with confidence for the translation of humane learning into moral wisdom, for the rational soul's reign over the mutinous realm of appetite and passion; and that is the main theme of his tragedies and strongly colours his great version of Homer. Greville, weighed down by his Calvinistic view of fallen man, goes beyond Chapman and even beyond Davies in his distrust of mere knowledge, although, like Chapman, he demands learning that is purified, active, and useful. Greville's philosophical and religious earnestness turns even *Caelica* into the least amorous of sonnet sequences. One bit may be quoted (from Sonnet LXXXVIII), partly for comparison with Donne's 'At the round earth's imagined corners':

> *The flood that did, and dreadful fire that shall,*
> *Drown, and burn up the malice of the earth,*
> *The divers tongues, and Babylon's downfall,*
> *Are nothing to the man's renewed birth:*
> *First, let the Law plough up thy wicked heart,*
> *That Christ may come, and all these types depart.*

For a concluding survey of the Elizabethan age we may turn back to Edmund Spenser (1552?–99), who, in the unified breadth of his culture and the bulk, variety, and centrality of his accomplishment, is the most complete representative of the English Renaissance.

The Shepherd's Calendar (1579) was the manifesto, as 'E. K.' made clear in his prefaces and notes, of a new poet. In beginning with pastorals Spenser was following the career sanctified by Virgil and others, and he was naturalizing in English the manner and themes of the convention, among them ecclesiastical satire. But, with all his exoticism, Spenser groups his twelve eclogues under the title of an old rural almanac and sets up Chaucer as his tutelary genius; and (like the poets of the Pléiade) he revives old words. Everywhere, as E. K. points out, the new poet observes decorum, that is, harmonious fitness of material, persons, language, tone; thus we have the high strains of *October* on heroic poetry and the *November* elegy, the half-elegant, half-rustic lyric to Elizabeth as the pastoral queen, the rude diction and metre of fable and satire. And almost every poem is a metrical experiment; the new poet, moreover, has a new sense of prosodic stress.

Spenser's minor poems of the early 1590's extend his sway over most provinces of Renaissance verse. *Mother Hubberd's Tale* is a comprehensive and pungent satire; as we might expect, Spenser uses the medieval beast-fable (and a decorously low style), not the classical manner that was to be adopted by Donne, Hall, and Marston. Satire on the corruptions of the court is one of many elements in the pastoral, *Colin Clout's Come Home Again*. *Muiopotmos*, the delicately embroidered tale of the fly and the spider, may be a fable of 'the poet and the politician', but its mock-heroic and pictorial charm is independent of ulterior meanings. The *Four Hymns*, on earthly and heavenly beauty and love, are the most elaborate— if not a systematic—exposition of Christian Platonism in our early poetry. Spenser is sincere in both his amatory idealism and his tender feeling for the human story of the Redeemer—motives that are fused in one of the best of the *Amoretti*, 'Most glorious

Lord of life', written for Easter. The sonnets in general, however, lack concentration and salience—Spenser's genius needed ampler room—and their virtues are gathered up, and heightened, in the *Epithalamion.*

Few of the world's great love-poems are associated with marriage, fewer still with a middle-aged poet's second marriage, but we may think the *Epithalamion* the most beautiful and satisfying love-poem in the language. (The *Prothalamion* has, in comparison, the external and dream-like beauty of pure art.) Even in this most personal poem Spenser is the consciously European artist. The Italian canzone is merged with the classical and Renaissance wedding-ode. The series of panel pictures, which follows the proceedings of the day from before sunrise to the rise of the moon, forms a processional pageant or masque of Hymen, and the stately pattern and rhythm, the refrain, and the tone of the whole are ritualistic. The actual wedding could hardly have been such a grand affair; Spenser puts in all the customs and ceremonies that literary and popular tradition, Roman and Irish, could supply, and weaves them into a tapestry both sumptuous and homely. In the total impression marriage is a supreme example of the beauty of order. The *Epithalamion* is indeed a metaphysical poem, however remote from *The Ecstasy* or *To his Coy Mistress.* The love of two ordinary persons is felt as a part, a splendid part, of the creative process of a divine world, and all nature shares in the glorious nuptial. The poet-bridegroom is so filled with love and wonder that the world is transfigured; even the 'trouts and pikes' of the river Mulla are superlative fish. And Elizabeth

Boyle is not simply Elizabeth Boyle but the eternal bride. She comes forth from her chamber like the sun of the 19th Psalm. Her snowy neck is like a marble tower, as in the Song of Songs. At the climax of religious adoration,

> *Open the temple gates unto my love,*
> *Open them wide that she may enter in,*

the poet has created such an atmosphere of reverent awe that he can without profanation echo another Psalm: 'Lift up your heads, O ye gates; and be ye lift up, ye everlasting doors; and the King of glory shall come in.' Yet this devout idealism is rooted in normal experience through its touches of actuality (Irish music, shouting boys, bellyfuls of wine), its ardour of sensuous desire, and the final hope of 'a large posterity'.

That huge fragment, *The Faerie Queene* (1590–96), with all its artistic and philosophical complexities, requires a book, not a page or two. The poem has long suffered from both one-sided praise and unjust disparagement; the romantic nineteenth century saw only its decorative romanticism, and for the 'metaphysical' twentieth it hardly exists at all. Spenser's ethical and allegorical aims have appeared merely wrongheaded, and this bias has distorted the appreciation of even his aesthetic qualities.

Some elements of Renaissance ideology have been touched upon already, such as the principles of Christian humanism, the didactic view of poetry, the doctrine *ut pictura poesis*, and these and other articles of the creed are united in Spenser. He saw the whole body of heroic poetry, from Homer to

Ariosto and Tasso, as philosophy teaching by examples, and his theory was fully shared by his contemporaries and his chief disciple, Milton; it is shared by modern novelists, if not by modern poets and critics. *The Faerie Queene* was not an escapist dream, it was a call to high ideals and high endeavour, a Renaissance conduct-book in verse; and it was typical of Christian humanism that the spectrum of virtues treated should range from Holiness to Courtesy. Spenser did, to be sure, create an ultra-romantic world of knights and ladies and magicians and monsters (a world which, whether we value it or not, lives in our imagination), but everywhere the romantic and preternatural are mixed with the homely and the real. Spenser's store of bright-eyed ladies remind us of Juliet and Desdemona, Imogen and Perdita; they have, in varying proportions, the unearthly beauty of symbols combined with feminine tenderness, strength, and loyalty. He needs to be read as the sage and serious and very human poet he was, and as the great artist he was.

Whatever the order of composition of the larger and smaller units, in the poem as it stands the first two books, of Holiness and Temperance, have the structure of a morality play, a pilgrim's progress; in the other four, especially the last three, the stories and groups shift and blend in the manner of Ariosto. Further, after the first book, Spenser tends to move away from strict allegory, from narrative with a double meaning, to the use of ethical types of character in various situations, as in modern novels.

In the Book of Holiness, conventions of medieval romance are raised to the religious plane. The traditional 'unpromising hero' becomes the untried

Christian soldier, who is led astray from true faith
(Una), falls into sensual sloth and pride, is saved by
grace (Arthur), and, though tempted to suicide in the
great scene with Despair, undergoes purification and,
a true St. George, accomplishes his quest, the slaying
of the dragon of sin. (The historical allegory is too
uncertain to go into.) The knight has at first the
blindness of a Kafka hero, but he attains a vision of
truth and right; one moving incident is his reluctant
return, after the ascent of the hill of contemplation,
to the world of evil and struggle. The last stage of his
quest may illustrate the way in which allegory passes
into symbolism like that of *The Waste Land*. After
the first day's battle the knight is refreshed by water
from a well; it is the 'pure river of water of life,
clear as crystal, proceeding out of the throne of God
and of the Lamb' (Rev. xxii, 1).[1] After the second
day, he is revived by fruit from the tree of life—'To
him that overcometh will I give to eat of the tree of
life, which is in the midst of the Paradise of God'
(Rev. ii, 7). The dragon is Satan, as in Revelation;
the three days of battle are a romance convention
and also the period of Christ's harrowing of hell.
When the knight is brought into the city

> *With shaumes, and trompets, and with clarions*
>   *sweet;*
> *And all the way the joyous people sings,*
> *And with their garments strowes the paved street,*

we think of Christ's entry into Jerusalem. Now the
victor over evil may for the first time see Una's face

[1] Since verbal echoes are not in question, this and following
texts are quoted from the familiar King James Bible—although
as a matter of fact these are almost completely identical with
the versions in the Geneva and Bishops' Bibles.

unveiled; and she is 'arrayed in fine linen, clean and white', 'for the marriage of the Lamb is come, and his wife hath made herself ready' (Rev. xix, 7–8). Thus, out of the staple materials of romance, and with a multitude of significant details, Spenser created a religious myth.

The Christian virtue of Holiness receives special treatment. The other virtues belong to the world of nature, of classical and Renaissance ethics— although the hero of Temperance, who starts with Platonic and Aristotelian wisdom, must in a crisis be rescued by grace. It is also typical of Spenser and his age that, whereas Chaucer, with all his scruples, could depict the uncanonical love of Troilus and Criseyde sympathetically, Spenser presents courtly love as wholly evil. It is no less typical that his heroine of Chastity is dedicated, not to virginity, but to the quest of the man she loves and is to marry. When, by the way, the two meet in combat, the poet's candid realism and idealism come together: Britomart, red-faced and sweating, is still so lovely that Artegall falls back 'And of his wonder made religion'.

The sensuous richness of Spenser has for many readers blurred his less obvious subtlety. Thus romantic criticism has seen in the Bower of Bliss (II, xii) an instinctively voluptuous poet letting himself go in a riot of the senses and then paying lip-service to virtue in the destruction of the Bower. If that were so, the normally orthodox poet would be violating the conception of Circe that ran from Homer through Ariosto and Tasso and Milton. More important is the positive fact that he uses his eclectic wealth of sensuous and sensual material with suggestive discrimination. As C. S. Lewis has shown, the picture is one of pathological sensuality based on two main lines of contrast, between the evil beauty of luxurious artifice and the pure beauty of simple nature, and between the unhealthy lust of the eye and the full fruition of honourable love. Compared with the Garden of Adonis (III, vi), or with the *Epithalamion*, the air of the Bower is heavy with corruption.

The Garden of Adonis begins with the miraculous conception of Belphoebe and Amoret, and perhaps nothing in English poetry makes the reader feel so drenched with sunlight. (In *The Faerie Queene*, as in *Paradise Lost*, light is a constant symbol of purity.) The twins are found by Venus and Diana; here Spenser joins two decorative myths, of the hue and cry after Cupid and Actaeon. Since Amoret is brought up by Venus in the natural paradise of the Garden, Spenser offers a biological myth of the endless cycle of generation. Then the theme is repeated in the myth of Venus and Adonis; their eternal love represents matter for ever receiving form. The Garden of Adonis is related to the fragment on Mutability, which, in its mythological symbolism, its varied display of Spenser's artistic powers, and its total import, is perhaps the most impressive part of the whole poem. In the last stanza we hear the inmost voice of a deeply troubled poet. He longs to believe, and does believe, the traditional doctrine of the world's evolving, under Providence, towards perfection, and yet the undeniable sway of Mutability on earth wrings his heart and evokes an impassioned prayer for the changeless peace and order of heaven.

The Faerie Queene is not all on the level of these few passages, though a multitude of other fine things could be cited. What frightens off the modern reader is not the legendary terrors of allegory, which is as essential in Spenser as in Dante, but the mere length and complexity of the poem. Yet the many great episodes would not achieve their effect without the aggregation of detail; Spenser must be allowed the scope and method of a novelist. And though the stanza he invented may seem at first to embody only a uniform and continuous flow of melody, the attentive reader will observe constant rhythmical modulations adapted to the various kinds of description, action, and dialogue. The archaisms of diction, which offended Ben Jonson (and which would be less conspicuous if Spenser were read, like Shakespeare and others, in modernized spelling), are more of an asset than a liability. Language and rhythm go along with imagination in maintaining an aesthetic distance, a variable yet consistent atmosphere and tone that create a world. Finally, we may remember that no poet has had greater or more varied disciples, Milton, Dryden, Wordsworth, Keats, and a host of others, and that Spenser is, more than any other individual, the father of English poetry.

We have noted some religious, philosophical, and literary principles that were a general inheritance, and, before we move into the next age, we may take a retrospective glance at a few more technical matters. The Tudor Englishman was patriotically and sometimes pathetically eager that the English language and literature should attain a place, if not with Latin and Greek (that could hardly be hoped), at least with Italian and French; and, though poetic genius was the gift of God, learning and discipline could do much. One common possession of writers and readers in the sixteenth and seventeenth centuries, a possession quite alien to us, was a training in formal rhetoric. If we think of the early poets as 'just writing', with due regard to rhyme and scansion, we should look into the formidable analysis of tropes and figures in George Puttenham's *Art of English Poesy* (1589). Since almost every writer and reader was brought up on Latin, one large element of poetic discipline and pleasure was the adaptation and recognition of traditional devices.

During the sixteenth century the language grew with extraordinary rapidity, and the latter half was punctuated by the cracklings of the 'ink-horn' controversy. One party welcomed the free addition to English of words from other tongues, ancient and modern; but purists, fearing (in the phrase of E. K.) 'a gallimaufray or hodgepodge of al other speches', would have the language grow from within, from the native stock. Providence brought about an English compromise. As the Book of Common Prayer and the Bible had already demonstrated, the special power and beauty of English were to spring from its combinations of Anglo-Saxon brevity, weight, and strength with the sonority, speed, and connotative richness of classical polysyllables.

In this connexion, to anticipate, we may note the beginnings, in such works as *The Faerie Queene*, Sylvester's popular translation of Du Bartas, and George Sandys' version of the *Metamorphoses*, of the 'poetic diction' that was to reach its artistic height in Milton and, during its long decline, to spread all over the eighteenth century. Saturation in Latin verse and verse-making led, not unnaturally, to the transferring to English of Latin idioms—the *Gradus* epithet, adjectives in place of adverbs, extensive employment of participles, the use of Latin derivatives in their literal sense (e.g. 'error' for 'wandering'). Along with such devices went generic abstractions, taken partly from Latin, partly from the language of science, which, while vitalized at first by specific purposes, came ultimately to be a lifeless convention. Thus, as Mr. Tillotson has pointed out, the 'finny drove' of *Comus* (line 115) directs our visual imagination to multitudinous fins waving in the moonlight; later, as a rule, such a phrase is merely a collective term or elegant euphemism.

The debates over classical metres grew out of motives similar to those behind the discussion of ink-horn words. In the latter half of the sixteenth century it was still possible to hold that English poetry, commonly based as it was on rhyme and syllable-counting, needed to be ordered and refined by the adoption of classical metrics. But existing confusion about English prosody heightened confusion and conflict over the acceptance of classical metrics *in toto* or of an accentual compromise. When we read Campion's somewhat belated essay and Daniel's reply (1602-3), we may be wholly on the side of Daniel's appeal to the native tradition and genius, but we should recognize that Campion's plea was limited and not irrational. In spite of the achievements of the later Elizabethan poets, Campion, a composer as well as a classicist, saw the need for more sophisticated principles, for the complex adjustments of metrical, syllabic, and rhetorical stress—principles that help to explain the delicate rhythms of his own rhymed lyrics and remind us, in a general way, of the great advances in technical mastery and subtlety that were now being made.

The variety of stanzaic patterns, which soon became infinite, defies brief description, but two great prosodic instruments may and must be given a word. The evolution of blank verse from Surrey to Milton, an evolution partly epitomized in Shakespeare, can be briefly summarized. In early or unsophisticated blank verse the dominant unit is the single, end-stopped line, and, though Surrey and other pioneers do have run-on lines, such verse may be little more than a sequence of unrhymed pentameters or couplets. But in parts of Marlowe and, with the most elaborate and intricate orchestration in the mature Shakespeare and Milton, the line is a variable and subordinate unit in a verse paragraph of unlimited modulations.

The other metrical form is the heroic couplet, not now of the Chaucerian kind (which is hardly felt as a couplet), but the closed couplet with balanced and often antithetical half-lines that was to culminate in Pope. Blank verse had originated as an equivalent for the hexameter, and the couplet owed much of its early development to translation and imitation of the Latin elegiac distich, Ovid's in particular. Among other contributions to the growth of the couplet was Edward Fairfax's *Godfrey of Bulloigne*, which had an influence attested by Waller and Dryden; it was in *ottava rima*, but Fairfax's handling of the whole stanza and of its final couplets was important. In the moulding of the couplet, as in other things, Jonson was a main force. And some practitioners stood outside the development of balanced smoothness; Donne's bold irregularity, in his satires, elegies, and *Anniversaries*, was very much his own.

The so-called Spenserians, Michael Drayton, Giles and Phineas Fletcher, William Browne, and George Wither, wrote in the age of Donne and Jonson, and some of them—like some of the Georgians—were resentfully conscious of an over-intellectual and alien world. The Spenserians—except the latest and greatest, Milton—inherited only provinces or parishes of the master's domain. We can find mild pleasure in Wither's pastoralism; we all know Browne's concise epitaph on the Countess of Pembroke and may have been led through Keats to dip into the diffuse *Britannia's Pastorals*. Not much leads us to Phineas Fletcher, but his brother's baroque poem, *Christ's Victory and Triumph* (1610), is a landmark between Southwell and Milton and Crashaw. The most versatile, voluminous, and generally attractive poet of the group is Drayton, whose industry covered the forty years before his death (1631). His early *Endymion and Phoebe* and his famous sonnet of 1619 (not his only good one) have already been mentioned. Though he remained an Elizabethan to the end, Drayton was in his way a conscientious artist not unresponsive to the growing refinement of craftsmanship. We cherish the forthright heroic odes on Agincourt and the Virginian voyage, the mock-heroic vivacity of *Nymphidia*, and the buoyant freshness and grace of his late pastoral verse, *The Muses' Elysium*. And some have relished the national and local patriotism of the huge and heterogeneous

Poly-Olbion. Drayton is not the kind of poet upon whom critics fix a microscopic eye, but he remains the sturdy bard of both heroic and merry England.

Apart from the conservative and relatively inconspicuous Spenserians, the dominant poetical modes of the earlier seventeenth century are of course represented by Jonson and Donne and their followers, that is, by the 'cavalier' and 'metaphysical' poets. Neither of the labels is very accurate or happy. If, when political cleavage developed, Jonson's numerous 'sons' were active or passive royalists, so were almost all other poets, including the metaphysicals and Waller and Denham. And if such courtiers as Carew, Suckling, and Lovelace fulfil our notion of cavalier poets, they were all disciples of Donne as well as of Jonson (and Herrick was neither a courtier nor a Donnian). Further, no definition of 'metaphysical' fits all of even the half-dozen chief poets who are so grouped. One suggestive fact is that, while there is a gulf between the typical Jonson and the typical Donne, a few poems have been assigned to both authors and are indeed much alike. In short, there are not two distinct schools; there are only a crowd of individual poets who in varying ways and degrees partake of the elements of sensibility and technique that are divided or shared between Jonson and Donne. Poets of both kinds as a rule turn away from the long, old-fashioned works of the Spenserians to concentrate, with a new artistic pressure, upon short poems and lyrics; their main themes are the love of woman and the love or fear of God.

The neo-classicism of Sidney was that of an aristocratic and eclectic amateur of the Renaissance, and

Elizabethan writing generally absorbed more romantic than neo-classical influence from Italy, France,
and Spain. Ben Jonson (1572–1637), the first great
neo-classical theorist and dictator and the first real
'man of letters' (though he had fought abroad and
killed an actor in a duel), was almost untouched by
continental vernacular literature and drew directly
from the ancients and their Neo-Latin expositors
and imitators. He shared the ethical and especially
Stoic ideals of serious humanism; witness such poems
as *Epode, To the World,* and the one famous stanza
of the Pindaric ode on Cary and Morison—not to
mention the commonplace-book, *Discoveries.* But
Jonson illustrates the humanist-poet's capacity both
for weighty observations on life and for little jewels
of art remote from life, and we identify him with his
lyrics (many of them from the plays and masques)
and non-satirical epigrams; these last, like Martial's,
include addresses to friends and epitaphs. One
difference between Jonson and Shakespeare is
exemplified by 'Come, my Celia' and 'O mistress
mine'. Both are variations on the universal theme,
Carpe diem, and both are consecutive arguments; but
Shakespeare's song is pastoral, popular, and 'artless'
and Jonson's is a sophisticated, particularized, and
less obviously singable paraphrase of Catullus.
Another kind of contrast is suggested by *A Hymn to
God the Father*; the movement, and some phrases,
may make us think of Herbert's *Discipline*, but
Jonson's earnest prayer has only hints of Herbert's
metaphorical and paradoxical texture. In general,
Jonson's lyrics and epigrams show the virtues and the
limitations of the pure neo-classical artist. On the one
hand we find intellectual and emotional rationality

and control, lucid and logical symmetry (even in the organizing of such borrowed conceits as compose 'Drink to me only with thine eyes'), and plain English enriched by felicitous echoes of the classics. On the other hand, we are rarely so stirred that we forget the conscious manipulation of fancy and word and rhythm by the skilled artificer. Amorous rapture and paternal grief are alike tender and graceful, detached and impersonal.

Robert Herrick (1591–1674), like other 'sons' of Ben, has a narrower poetical range and nothing of Jonson's ethical humanism. The pieties of *Noble Numbers* express more satisfaction than struggle. The title of the secular poems, *Hesperides*, suggests both the precious golden fruit of Herrick's classical art and his blending of ancient allusion with the 'May-poles, hock-carts, wassails, wakes' of Devonshire; and what is, in some moods, 'the loathed West', is normally the pastoral Arcadia of Elizabethan song. In his clerical exile from London and tavern symposia, Herrick can labour with Horatian patience to perfect his verses. In the dozens of little poems on his seraglio of dainty mistresses he carries Jonson's cool amatory art into further, one might almost say feminine, delicacies of phrase and rhythm. Now and then there is something like metaphysical wit, though it is effortless and unobtrusive—'That liquefaction of her clothes', 'Thy Protestant to be'. And sometimes fancy rises to the plane of imagination. If we put the *Night Piece to Julia* beside what may have inspired it, Jonson's 'The fairy beam upon you', we see that in Jonson's simple dramatic song the items are merely listed, while in Herrick Julia's beauty becomes the centre of the natural world. A

perhaps better comparison is afforded by Jonson's
'Still to be neat, still to be drest' and Herrick's
Delight in Disorder. The former is a little whole of
generalized and almost prosaic statement in which
no detail calls attention to itself; Herrick's piece is a
tissue of visual particulars which are miniature paradoxes. And while Jonson sets wholesome nature
against artifice, Herrick's praise is given to the artificial simulation of nature, and in the end his figurine
lady becomes herself a symbol of charming 'wanton-
ness' as opposed to virtuous propriety. In a very
different context Corinna, that 'sweet slug-a-bed',
becomes a somewhat parallel symbol. This elaborate
poem celebrates the merry ritual of May Day, and,
though details seem both conventional and casual,
they work subtle variations on the contrasts between
civilization and nature, Christian morality and
paganism, and finally—with a sombre echo of
Catullus—between amorous youth and age and death.
The same theme, more lightly treated, is still more
familiar in 'Gather ye rose-buds while ye may'; and
the immediate and lasting popularity of the lyric
attests the perfect expression that Herrick could
give to commonplaces.

We must take for granted the man-of-the-world
insouciance and sprightly humour of 'Natural, easy
Suckling', and the exalted spirit of love and honour
that kindled the best-known poems of the ideal
cavalier, Richard Lovelace, and the poetry of many
other men who deserve their place in the anthologies. Thomas Carew (1594/5-1640) perhaps best
exemplifies the assimilation of a metaphysical strain
by a Jonsonian amorist. His *Elegy* on Donne—one of
the period's few really critical essays—glorifies the

older poet's revolt against shallow classicism and
his original, tough, masculine wit and style. Such
appreciative insight prepares us for more of Donne in
Carew's own verse than we may observe, though
much is there. In general, and even in *A Rapture*,
Carew refines and strengthens the attitudes of the
conventional lover through his formal and stylistic
elegance. His poems are preconceived wholes, not
immediate experiences. Touches of wit are subdued
to the dominant pattern and tone, and metaphorical is combined with logical symmetry. Thus
To my Inconstant Mistress begins with 'thou, poor
excommunicate' and ends with 'thy false apostasy'.
A Deposition from Love carries a military metaphor
from the opening 'your rebel sex' to the final 'deposed
kings'. In the famous 'Ask me no more where Jove
bestows', successive—and traditional—metaphorical
hyperboles, in parallel structure and sonorous
rhythm, elevate the woman of a lover's compli-
ments into a cosmic vision. But Carew can be best
enjoyed in occasional tastes; all his technical resources
cannot disguise monotony.

If the typical cavalier lyric is an ideal, impersonal
creation of pure art, much metaphysical poetry is an
exploration of individual experience set forth with
expressive originality and immediacy. The development of such poetry was indeed a chronological and
ideological parallel to the anti-Ciceronian movement
in prose, which grew out of sceptical, empirical, and
scientific distrust of the traditional verities and
traditional 'public' style. The metaphysical temper
or manner appears more distinctive to us—at least
to those of us who think they can define it—than it
did to its own age, which referred loosely to 'wit' and

'strong lines'. William Drummond, a follower of continental and conservative fashions, censured the new warping of the European tradition into 'metaphysical ideas and scholastic quiddities', and Dryden popularized the term in that general sense. The first full analysis came from Dr. Johnson in his life of Cowley (1779): he emphasized the violent yoking of unlike ideas and images, the straining after intellectual subtlety, originality, particularity, and recondite learning. Though Johnson's neo-classical standpoint is not ours, nor his hierarchy of metaphysical poets, his discussion remains the *locus classicus* which we can modify as we choose. Modern definitions have added or redefined various elements and qualities: a philosophic consciousness; the fusion of thought and feeling, and of seriousness and ironic wit; internal tension and conflict; the active revelation of complex mental processes rather than the presentation of a finished result; the language and rhythms of speech instead of the 'poetical'; the realistic or erudite rather than the fanciful or mythological image, and the functional and organic rather than the ornamental or illustrative use of it; and so on. But, as we observed before, no definition covers poets so diverse as Chapman, the two Herberts, Crashaw, Vaughan, Traherne, Cowley, Marvell, and others. Not only are some of these doubtfully metaphysical names, but there is metaphysical writing elsewhere, for example, in Shakespeare's plays, sonnets, and, in quintessence, in the enigmatic *Phoenix and the Turtle*.

During this past generation the rediscovery of the metaphysicals has had a large share in giving poetry and criticism a new direction. In doing so it has often led to excessive and exclusive claims for the meta-physical virtues and to needless and uncritical denigration of other modes. Many of the claims and definitions are based chiefly on Donne (1572–1631), and some need qualification even in regard to him. If a philosophical poet is one who, like Chapman, has a coherent philosophy to expound, Donne was not a philosophical poet, though he made constant use of philosophical ideas. He did not banish 'rhetoric', he inaugurated a new kind; or rather, he carried into the poetry of love the colloquial, dramatic, ironic realism that decorum had reserved for satire. If he fused thought and feeling, he did not always maintain the fusion through even a short poem, but could lapse into logical hair-splitting. Donne is a much smaller and in some ways less complex poet than Spenser. His technique is exciting but, once grasped, is fairly obvious, and other rewards are not inexhaustible, whereas Spenser continually reveals new depths and overtones.

Whether or not the young man about town was as loose as the poet made himself out to be, Donne was not a mere libertine but a curious explorer of the relations of body and soul—his own body and soul, since he has little interest in women's feelings except as they affect his. The question of personal involvement, or of philosophical seriousness, is further complicated by Donne's dramatic method and his varying admixture of wit and levity; we remember the *Paradoxes and Problems* which devote specious ingenuity to the support of any unorthodox proposition. One of his tricks is the turning of accepted ideals upside down—as when constancy in love is a vice or heresy. His moods

range from the witty defence of promiscuity, or the
denial of anything but physical satisfaction, to sober
argument for the interrelations of soul and body or
for love as a self-sufficient good, the supreme good.
On this last level he can outdo the Petrarchans in
hyperbole, but he is convincing through his ironic
indirectness, realistic particularity, ratiocination,
and explosive force. In such an unconventional
aubade as *The Sun Rising*, the great source of light
and life merely regulates the workaday world; the
real centre of the real world is the lovers' bed, and
their love transcends time. The same theme receives
fuller treatment in *The Canonization*: the private
world of love reduces bustling careerists to insigni-
ficance, and in the quiet conclusion, so different from
the violent opening, the ideal lovers are invoked as
saints. On a still higher plane of idealism are several
poems that Donne presumably addressed to his wife
(the two poems just mentioned may have been also).
'Sweetest love, I do not go' makes it clear that he
can, when he wishes, combine tension with tenderness, argument with lyrical melody. *A Valediction:
Forbidding Mourning* implies a completeness of
relationship between man and woman, and between
soul and body, that needs no proof; the images are
illustrative rather than argumentative. (The famous
conceit or 'emblem' of the compasses—which may
have been derived from Guarini—is more elaborate
than typical of Donne's scientific images.) And there
is complete security, with no hint of doubt or
laborious demonstration, in the grand style and
sweeping rhythms of *The Anniversary*, in which love
conquers both time and death.

Donne's two *Anniversaries* (1611–12), written

nominally in memory of his patron's young daughter, Elizabeth Drury, should be read along with the *Cantos of Mutability*, *Nosce Teipsum*, *The Tears of Peace*, and the *Treatie of Humane Learning*. Like Spenser, Davies, Chapman, and Greville, Donne is, in an age of growing scepticism and confusion, taking stock of the human situation. He differs from the other poets in mind and method and in his keener and fuller knowledge of scientific discoveries and speculations; a further source of pessimism is the widespread doctrine of the decay of nature and man as the world approaches its dissolution. Donne does not share Chapman's humanistic faith; he is more akin to the others, especially Greville, in his dark view of fallen, helpless man, his ignorant pretensions to knowledge, and his need of grace. Elizabeth Drury, like Christ or the Virgin in Roman Catholic meditations, is the symbol of the perfection that man has lost. True knowledge, true salvation from sin, can be attained only in religion and another life. As usual, Donne expresses general ideas and attitudes through vividly realized particulars. The obverse side of that power—which appears even in his short poems—is inadequate control of tangential details. Although, as Mr. Martz has shown, the *Anniversaries* are deliberately ordered religious exercises, the *First* especially suffers from the difficulties inherent in the symbolism and from awkward articulation of the parts. In the *Second* Donne moves more freely.

Intellectually, Donne had always been a Christian, but his progress toward assurance was hindered by his sense of Roman Catholic outlawry, his shift to the Church of England, his moral lapses, the worldly disaster of his marriage, and his restless mind. His earlier religious poems, though not without the true accent, were in the main composed in his intellect. Apart from the *Anniversaries*, it was chiefly in the early sonnets and the hymns written after his wife's death (1617) that the intensity of his religious experience received utterance. The worn, ascetic Dr. John Donne has the same sensibility and technique as Jack Donne, egocentric and dramatic violence, passionate ratiocination, concrete particularity— and occasional ugliness—of imagery, simplicity of language and complication of idea, ironic wit, boldly expressive irregularities of rhythm. But now the conflicts and tensions spring from his agonized consciousness of sin, his fear of death and divine justice, his desperate faith in the redeeming sacrifice of Christ. The great Fundamentalist drama is enacted in the poet's intense imagination, and centred in himself. For the lover of women the every- day world had ceased to exist; now it weighs upon the earth-bound man who cries for salvation. The lover could triumphantly affirm love's conquest of time; now he faces judgment and eternity—'What if this present were the world's last night?' The macabre strain that touched even poems of love has full play in the sinner's preoccupation with death— though in the *Hymn to God, my God, in my Sickness* he feels at last something of calm security, and, flat on his bed like a map, can see his 'west'.

In comparison with the violent Donne, the quieter intensity and quieter art of his young friend George Herbert (1593–1633) may not take us by storm. Yet the poetry of Herbert is a record of religious experience more central and comprehensive, and more humble, than Donne's, a record of strivings, failures, and victories in the practice of the Christian life. A number of poems, to be sure, come from the parish priest of Bemerton—these are indeed the classical picture of the beauty of order in the Caroline church—but the many greater poems are universal. Herbert finds his themes in his own heart, in his efforts to subdue his high, worldly, rebellious spirit to the divine will or to rekindle the inner flame when it seems to flicker low. What makes Herbert a great religious—and metaphysical—poet is this conflict and tension; and even when he is intimately personal the poems are an impersonal mirror in which anyone who would live above the natural level may see himself. Nor is Herbert one of the sour saints; he is a lover of music and of 'mirth'. Sometimes, happily, he feels his shrivelled heart recover its greenness, and then he can smell the dew and rain 'And relish versing'.

Herbert's art is neat and subtle, and—to borrow his adjectives for the Lord's 'returns'—fresh, sweet, and clean. His stanzaic and metrical experimentation is of remarkable range, but he is avowedly devoted to plain language and he rarely raises his voice. Once in a while, as in the dramatically violent opening of *The Collar*, he may remind us of Donne, but even that poem is entirely developed in his own way. Though he was a scholar and, like many men of his age, wrote Latin and Greek verse, his images are drawn largely from everyday life and the Bible; some of his little shocks of surprise come from his use of idioms of business and law in regard to the soul's dealings with God—for instance, in the sonnet *Redemption*. Herbert is conspicuously fond of the emblematic technique. The sixteenth and early

seventeenth centuries produced, all over Europe,
hundreds of emblem books, in which allegorical and
symbolic pictures were interpreted in a versified
gloss, and the fashion affected many English poets.
One famous example is Herbert's 'Love bade me
welcome', an allegorical anecdote of Love enter-
taining a dusty, sinful traveller who hesitates to
accept such hospitality. Bountiful love on one side,
guilty reluctance on the other, are conveyed not
only in words and implications but in quick and
positive, hovering and broken rhythms; and several
climactic turns in the dialogue lead to one of Herbert's
simple, final understatements, 'So I did sit and eat'.
On its first level of meaning, the poem is an emblem
of the Eucharist; more broadly, it is a picture of
God's infinite love for erring man. Whatever their
themes and manner and length, Herbert's best poems
are organized wholes. Usually his battles are fought
under our eyes, and the issue may be in doubt, yet
every image, line, and phrase contributes to the
developing pattern; there is no fumbling or rambling.
The familiar *Virtue* is detached and reflective rather
than dramatic or analytical; after a series of illustrative contrasts, metaphysical wit condenses a life
of conflict, and its reward, into the brief, homely,
and tremendous image of the last lines. But unity
and simplicity do not exclude potent ambiguity.
At the end of *The Collar*, when the poet hears 'one
calling, "Child!"' the single word is a tender rebuke
of childish rebellion, a reminder of the former
relation of Father and son, and a forgiving anticipation of its renewal; moreover, that word and the
poet's reply give a new meaning to the title and the
whole poem.

If we base our definition of metaphysical poetry on Donne and Herbert, or on them and Marvell, it hardly touches Richard Crashaw (1612/13–49) and must be stretched to include Henry Vaughan (1621/2 –95). Read against the background of all English poetry, indeed, Crashaw seems to be a 'sport', although we recognize, in excess, Italianate and Spanish qualities that had appeared in some Elizabethans and in Giles Fletcher and the early religious verse of Donne. Crashaw, however, represents a later wave of more extravagant conceitism, and in his original as well as his translated work we may be more conscious of the un-English than of the English elements in his sensibility and poetic manner. The first editor of *Steps to the Temple* (1646) described Crashaw as 'Herbert's second, but equal, who hath retrieved poetry of late, and returned it up to its primitive use; let it bound back to heaven-gates, whence it came'. But resemblance ends with Crashaw's title and the fact of his writing sacred poetry (he wrote some secular and even amatory verse as well); and to move from Herbert to Crashaw is to leave the plain little church of Bemerton— 'Neither too mean nor yet too gay'—for the gaudy ornaments and pictures of Latin Catholicism. Without going into the manifold and confusing definitions of 'baroque'—which has become a terminological maid-of-all-work—we may get at a good part of its meaning for poetry by reading Crashaw. He can be plain and direct—'She's for the Moors and martyrdom'—or display a genuine if sophisticated tenderness in the *Nativity*, but his name suggests flights of flamboyant adoration. We see Christ, the Virgin Mary, Mary Magdalene,

St. Teresa, through dazzling and 'delicious' images of wounds, blood, fire, tears, doves. One element of baroque—which had appeared in Giles Fletcher—is the ringing of changes on the paradoxical contrasts between the humble life, suffering, and death of Christ and the saints and their real power and majesty. Then there is the use of sexual images in devotional poetry, which is far older than the Counter-Reformation, though Crashaw's rapturous intensity is his own. It is a long way from 'I sing of a maiden' to *The Weeper* or *The Flaming Heart*. If baroque form is a matter of dynamic association and movement rather than the overt, logical organization of neoclassicism, it can easily lapse into formlessness. There is no apparent reason why *The Weeper* should not be half as long, or ten times as long, as it is; we should prefer the former alternative.

Herbert could hardly have had two disciples more different from himself and each other than Crashaw and Vaughan. Vaughan had a second birth in the two parts of *Silex Scintillans* ('Sparkling Flint') of 1650 and 1655. The very title, by the way, is an emblem. Vaughan's 'conversion' was a gradual deepening and concentration of his spiritual forces over a period of time; among the causes were the public and private sorrows of the Civil War, the death of his brother William and of his wife, his own illness, and study of the Bible and of Herbert, who had opened the way for religious poetry. Vaughan is the great exponent of Christian Neoplatonism in English, and in the nature of his vision he is linked, by affinity or debt, with the Neoplatonic and Hermetic traditions and with such more or less mystical spirits as Jacob Boehme, Sir Thomas Browne, and his own twin brother Thomas, whose Hermetic and alchemical writings afford some glosses to Henry's poems. Though Vaughan echoes Herbert constantly, more so perhaps than any English poet echoes another, his bond is rather religious than artistic; and he is akin to Herbert in his earnestly practical piety, his consciousness of man's and his own sinful will and weakness and of divine love. While the poems that stress th's theme are not his best, it is his central Christian faith that keeps Vaughan's mysticism from dissolving into the nebulous pantheism of some later 'mystics'. He differs widely from the non-mystical Herbert, and from most poets of the age (except Marvell and of course Traherne), in his religious feeling for nature. Though good Christians had the authority of Calvin and others as well as the Bible for God's revelation of himself in the secondary book of his works, few men of the seventeenth century— apart from some real scientists and some occultists —approached God through nature and their senses. Indeed the pure Neoplatonist would leave all material things behind in his spiritual ascent; but Vaughan delights to find the One in the Many. An exile on earth, he is happiest when he has a glimpse of the white purity of heaven, or of the presence of God in bird or tree or flower or stone.

Vaughan's mystical insights cannot well be rendered with the concrete precision that we regard as a metaphysical quality. He does use colloquial language, at times with magnificent effect—'I saw Eternity the other night'. But the special difficulties of his quest, of finding a form, imagery, and language for describing the indescribable, help to make Vaughan a notoriously uneven craftsman. Only a

few poems, such as *The Night*, are perfect wholes; even
in the famous, and short, *The Retreat*, the wording
is seldom inevitable and sometimes slipshod. In
general, and naturally enough, he is inclined to sink
or stumble between the moments of vision that bring
great phrases with them.

It is fitting that a sketch of cavalier and metaphysical poetry should end with the poet who best
combined the two traditions, Andrew Marvell
(1621–78). (We have to omit many fine poems struck
off by the lesser poets, from Henry King's softly
throbbing *Exequy* to such clever exercises in the
amatory fashion as Cowley's.) Marvell's best poems
were written apparently in the early 1650's. *The
Definition of Love* and *To his Coy Mistress* are
among the great metaphysical poems of love, but the
latter is also in the classical tradition, and both have
a spare, clean-cut symmetry and swift, supple sonority that are very different from the normally staccato
Donne; they are not more simple but they are under
impeccable control. The essence of both poems is
paradox, yet every idea and word is an integral part
of the pattern. The very title, *The Definition of Love*,
is paradoxical, and the infinity of frustrated love is
rendered in terms of the exact sciences of astronomy
and geometry. Even the phrase 'extended soul' is a
philosophical paradox, and the 'iron wedges' that
follow add a scientific connotation to the Horatian
image of fate. A degree of abstract Latinate diction
and the rhythm raise the poem from a lyrical to a
heroic level. *To his Coy Mistress* is the period's finest
variation on the theme of *Carpe diem*. A series of
witty, particular, hyperbolical fancies about unlimited space and time lead to the grim fact of

mortality, which is realized in phrases half general and suggestive, half particular and concrete; and the lover resolves the antithesis between love and death with the exhortation to use and conquer time. The poem has the precise logical sequence of a syllogism, yet it is filled with metaphysical reverberations. And with all the changes in tone and tempo, it has the unity and clarity, the ease and grace, of a cavalier lyric.

But Marvell feels other tensions than those of love. His religious and moral seriousness, his recognition of conflict between good and evil, appears directly in some poems and is between the lines in others; and it embraces opposed views of nature. For Marvell, as for Vaughan and Sir Thomas Browne, nature is the art of God, the God who makes the tropical paradise of Bermuda a clean Puritan temple. Nature is a world of quiet and innocence, a refuge and refreshment, yet it may be spoiled by corrupted man. Marvell is, however, no romantic primitivist. He is an intellectual and ethical being who, though his mind can annihilate 'all that's made To a green thought in a green shade', is always master of his experience and knows the limitations of such moods. His usually simple language and images accomplish miracles of suggestion, as in such an ostensibly slight poem as *The Garden*. At the same time Marvell can see nature as man's corrupter and destroyer. And ambivalent views of external as well as of human nature appear even in the *Horatian Ode upon Cromwell's Return from Ireland*, a classical and metaphysical poem which, for all its originality, comes closer to the heroic Horace than anything else in English.

The massive bulk, power, and complexity of John Milton (1608–74) can be surveyed only from a distance, through an 'optic glass'. To look back over the ground we have traversed, Milton's instincts and training kept him almost untouched by metaphysical influence—though we might ask, for instance, if 'Himself is his own dungeon' (*Comus*, line 385) is less metaphysical than Marvell's 'mine own precipice I go'. He conceived of poetry as 'more simple, sensuous, and passionate' than logic and rhetoric, but his terms, even if not misconstrued, are not an adequate description of his own work. Milton was, to put it roughly, a Spenserian who became the greatest of European neo-classical poets. In other words, he belonged to what had once been, and through him continued to be, the main stream of English poetry. Spenser was Milton's great forerunner both as artist and as the heroic poet of religious and ethical themes, and was (according to Dryden's report) his avowed master. He paid formal tribute to Shakespeare and Jonson, and echoed these and lesser predecessors. Milton moved rapidly from a thin and 'conceited' Elizabethan sweetness towards concentration, order, rationality, and restraint. *Comus* was a unified mosaic of the earlier and later styles of Milton and his whole century. The grand style of *Paradise Lost* emerged in *Lycidas* and the heroic sonnets of the Commonwealth period. But ornate grandeur was not the final phase. There followed the almost Biblical plainness of *Paradise Regained* and the rugged irregularity of *Samson Agonistes*. Thus Milton's art, after a few youthful poems, evolved within the classical tradition. But while a multitude of English and European poets became only mirrors of neo-classical convention, Milton's thought, feeling, imagination, and art were conspicuously dynamic and conspicuously his own. His mature poetry is not less complex than that of the metaphysicals but rather more so; its complexity, however, is further below the surface.

Most poets of the sixteenth and seventeenth centuries were, through the nature of their intellectual cultivation, not only English but European, and Milton was the greatest and the last master of that universal knowledge which the Renaissance demanded of the ideal poet and teacher. And if his art was born of the marriage of individual genius with all Western culture, from Homer and the Bible to his own time, it is no less fundamental that he was not merely an artist but, like the ancients and Dante, a citizen also. Among English and European poets Milton was also the greatest and last of Christian humanists. Even at Cambridge the young man had a vision, Platonic, Christian, and Baconian, of a new era in which free inquiry, the full resources of human and divine knowledge, would create the perfect society. To the fulfilment of that vision, and the Puritan ideal of the holy community, Milton gave his twenty best years and his eyesight. But by the time of *Paradise Lost* (1667) the poet, like the age, had altered. The central motive of the fall was Eve's yielding to Satan's offer of superhuman knowledge, and Milton's attitude towards such irreligious pride aligned him with Davies and Chapman and Greville and Donne rather than with the confident exponents of science.

Milton began as a serene and cloistered scholar more skilled in Latin than in English verse; he revealed, however, both an intensely sensuous temperament and the high ambitions of a poet-priest. His first great English poem, *On the Morning of Christ's Nativity*, written at the time of his twenty-first birthday, has its youthful exuberance, its Italianate conceits, but the sequence of themes is masterfully organized—the peaceful setting, the angelic music (which links the birth of Christ with the other two supreme events, creation and the judgment day), and the flight of the pagan gods; and the rhythm bears out the poet's triumphant joy in the union and order of heaven and earth. The *Nativity* is, for Milton, baroque. *L'Allegro* and *Il Penseroso* (1631?) are neo-classical in their formal patterns of parallel and contrast, in their generalized images, the harmonizing of all details into one central effect, the impersonal rendering of personal moods. We might say that the subdued lushness of the young Elizabethan has been chastened by the rational urbanity of Jonson, though the pupil already excels the master in his combination of civilized grace and freshness and evocative language and rhythms. There is some irony in the fact that the most famous picture of Merry England in English verse came from the great Puritan poet, the hammer of Church and King.

It was the religious humanist, the man of contemplation and action, who on his twenty-fourth birthday made the earnest resolve, with a prayer for sufficient grace, to live as ever in his great Taskmaster's eye. The first fruits of this renewed self-consecration were *On Time* and *At a Solemn Music* and the far longer hymn of adoration, *Comus* (1634). The best preface to *Comus*, and to most of Milton's

early poetry, is the account he later gave of the
growth of his youthful ideal of chastity and love.
Though he had delighted in the art of Ovid and his
fellows, he had turned from their sensual licence to
the idealism of Dante and Petrarch and the romances
of chivalry; then from 'the divine volumes of Plato'
he had gained higher insight into the love of knowledge and virtue; and above all there had been 'those
chaste and high mysteries' taught by St. Paul and
celebrated in Revelation. Thus *Comus* is, like other
works of Milton's, at once a private and a public
utterance. The Christian Platonism of the masque
has nothing to do with the Renaissance 'religion of
beauty in women' or with the spurious Platonics of
the Caroline court; as in *The Faerie Queene*, the pure
light of heaven illuminates active virtue on earth.
To the enchanter's libertine naturalism the Lady
replies at first on the level of the natural reason; but
then, with a 'sacred vehemence', she rises to the
religious plane in her exaltation of 'the sun-clad
power of Chastity', 'the sage And serious doctrine of
Virginity'. And in the epilogue the Attendant Spirit,
who is a guardian angel, recapitulates the same ideas
in allusive and partly Spenserian symbolism. It has
been observed that in Comus' speech on the bounties
of nature the images have a Shakespearian immediacy, and the result is an appropriate suggestion of
immoderate disorder; the normal texture is, so to
speak, composed in the single-minded assurance of
the harmonious order of God and nature.

The texture of *Lycidas* (1637) has the appearance
of similar 'precomposition', but beneath the smooth
surface there is conflict. The author of this poem has
experienced his first real shock. The drowning of a

Cambridge acquaintance rouses the poet to nothing less than the questioning of God's providence and justice: why should a man, why should John Milton, strive to fit himself for God's service when he may be cut off on the threshold? Emotional tension is at once heightened and controlled by the impersonal dramatic medium of the pastoral convention. The most heterogeneous and outwardly decorative details are woven into a whole of solid, objective density and complexity of suggestion. Thus, following the illusory solace of the passage on flowers, the tremendous surmises on the whereabouts of the tossing body imply—partly in their volume of sound—the helplessness of puny man against the elements that God could have restrained. In the end Milton reaffirms the answer he had reached a hundred lines earlier, but this assured trust in God and the conditions of earthly life comes to him only with the apocalyptic vision of the soul of Lycidas being welcomed into heaven. And the unearthly beauty of the vision carries the reader upward with the poet.

During most of the twenty years that Milton gave to the defence of liberty on many fronts, he had to forgo his dreams of the great heroic poem and be content with occasional sonnets—to friends, on public men and events, on his blindness and his 'late espoused saint'. Some remind us of the Horace of genial hospitality, some of the Horace of lofty patriotic odes. The public sonnets are both massive and fluid, and, as we observed before, they show features of Milton's developing epic manner. Periphrasis, for example, may be seen here, as in *Paradise Lost*, to be not automatic inflation but a method, no less fertile than metaphysical wit, of securing a variety of oblique effects. And the sonnet on the massacre in Piedmont, in spite of its especially arresting rhymes, is a structure of run-on lines and medial pauses that approaches the wheeling paragraphs of the epic.

The use of blank verse instead of rhyme for a heroic poem was a bold innovation, and Milton enlarged and refined its resources with equal splendour and subtlety. The iambic pentameter is a half-audible norm, providing both the pleasure of an expected pattern and the basis of unexpected and endless variations. The number of stresses varies from four to six or even more, and from the heavy to the light; the position and the weight of caesural pauses constantly shift; and while the line is felt as a rhythmical unit, the run-on lines and strong medial pauses tend to make another system of variable units that begin in one line and end in another. But a few bald statements about mechanics do not take us very far into Miltonic harmonies. Whether or not we scan and consider, much of the aesthetic effect, and even of the meaning, depends on our reading *Paradise Lost* aloud—and we can seldom take breath in less than twenty lines. Since the metrical necessities and possibilities of an epic differ greatly from those of dramatic speech, it is idle to compare Milton with Shakespeare.

That Milton's language and syntax are classical and un-English is a charge more often repeated than tested; one may simply read the poem and ask himself how many really un-English words and idioms he meets. Alleged classicisms are often only forcible condensations. Like most great poets, Milton takes daring liberties of all kinds, and, for the sake of distributing emphasis, pointing contrasts, and so forth, he can treat long periodic sentences, subsidiary clauses, and suspended phrases, with the freedom of Latin arrangement, but the meaning is hardly ever in doubt for a moment—though that meaning may carry implications and overtones that demand slower assimilation. One general characteristic of the poem, to which rhythm and diction both contribute, is the sweeping speed of its onward movement.

Decorum, 'the grand masterpiece to observe', was not, for a great poet, a negative rule; it was a dynamic principle. And a heroic poem, above all a poem on the fall of man, required a style of ritualistic elevation, a style that would lift the reader out of everyday feelings and affairs. So Milton wears his singing robes, as Homer and Virgil had done. But he does not wear buskins. Doubtless, if we think of the limpid fluidity of Chaucer or Spenser, the Miltonic manner may seem unduly heightened, even stiff; but can we conceive of *Paradise Lost* in the manner of Chaucer or Spenser (or Donne)? A realistic treatment of Adam and Eve would have made them a suburban pair practising nudism in the back garden; Milton kept them, and the rich beauties of Eden, at a requisite aesthetic distance. Even the universe is stylized; when Satan, at the gates of hell, looks out upon the warring elements of chaos, what he sees is the vast world of astronomy, but the terms of the description are traditional. Yet within the limits of stylization there is room for functional variety of language and rhythm and tone, as in the speeches of the debaters in hell, or in the humanizing of Satan before, and of Adam and Eve after, the fall. The grand archangel becomes an Iago or Iachimo; Adam and Eve, in the process of corruption, speak, not with the majestic dignity of immortal innocence, but in the accents of a half-human Mr. and Mrs. John Doe, calculating, persuading, lusting, quarrelling, repenting, pleading, and forgiving. Less obvious perhaps than stylized grandeur and energy, though not less important, are simplicity of expression and subtlety of suggestion. Nothing in metaphysical poetry, or in Dante, is more simply, complexly, and tragically suggestive in word and rhythm than the last lines, the picture of the now very human pair, with their blended feelings of sorrow, fear, and hope, leaving Eden to begin their life anew in the grim world of history.

Milton exploited to the full the opportunities for contrast—and at the same time for structural links—afforded by his fable, characters, scenes, and thematic ideas. We have noticed the earlier and later Adam and Eve, the earlier and later Satan. The great rebel is opposed, on different planes, to God, Christ, and Abdiel; heroic in hell, he shrinks in the world of good. Heaven and hell embrace manifold contrasts—some of them already used by Spenser—between light and darkness, good and evil, love and hate, bliss and pain, life and death, order and anarchy, freedom and servitude, humility and pride, reason and passion, creation and destruction. Eden has the pure beauty of nature, Pandemonium the meretricious beauty of artifice. And there are contrasts of implicit irony: we first look upon Eden as we accompany Satan into it, and the ensuing scenes of idyllic innocence are overshadowed by his presence. The oftener we read the poem, the more, and more minute, bonds of contrast and correspondence we find.

In addition to many learned or imaginative embellishments of Genesis, there were available the devices of the classical epics—celestial agencies, councils, recapitulation of the past and prophecy of the future. The many things, large and small, that Milton imitated from Virgil and Homer he re-created for his own purposes, from invocations of the Muse (which for him became prayers) to epic similes; no ancient simile has the complex, poignant beauty of 'Not that fair field of Enna', with its hinted parallel between Proserpine and Eve. As artist, Milton was humbly proud to link himself with the classical masters; as a Christian poet, he was always conscious of having a higher theme, and the merely heroic qualities of the epic hero he gave to Satan. At times even Milton could not altogether overcome the difficulty of handling such a story as his in the concrete terms of the heroic poem. The war in heaven is a dubious mixture of the material and the symbolic, though it has its great moments and rises steadily to the climactic onset of Christ in 'The chariot of Paternal Deity'. The nature of the heroic poem partly explains also why, in spite of Milton's efforts, God becomes at moments dynastic and hardly less legalistic than theology had made him. The poet is vehemently repudiating the Calvinistic Jehovah and vehemently proclaiming man's responsible freewill and God's providence and love; but, when God himself expounds the case, his voice, in a few disastrous lines, is that of John Milton arraigning the foes of righteousness. Elsewhere God can be a figure of divine sublimity.

But even if Milton's presentation of the forces of good is almost inevitably inadequate, we should not let that, along with his powerful presentation of evil, distort our view of his total conception. We must, when we begin the poem, assume that God represents perfect goodness, love, reason, order, whatever ideal absolutes we at least wish to believe in. If we start there, we shall not be carried away by Satan's first great speech of defiance, which so many romantic readers of the past and present have taken as splendidly heroic. Milton often uses the Elizabethan dramatic method, giving to characters speeches that violate the assured beliefs and convictions of the audience and that will be accordingly condemned; the poet could count on such beliefs and convictions in his early readers. When Satan denounces God as a wicked tyrant, a mere wielder of superior force, and sets himself up as an injured and righteous rebel, he is blaspheming all goodness and order and glorifying pride, passion, and anarchy. Here, and throughout (candid soliloquy excepted), Satan and his followers, being enveloped in spiritual blindness, are enveloped in dramatic irony. Obviously Milton had enough dramatic imagination to create the tremendous figure; we can hardly talk about the poet's self-projection unless we are prepared to give the same naïve verdict on Shakespeare and his villains. And the modern reaction against secular liberalism has made the spiritual climate much more favourable than it was a generation ago to the understanding of Milton's vision of order and humility. Even if we abandon theology (including the poet's bold heresies and metaphysical ideas), the poem remains a great and living myth of the war between good and evil in the world and in the soul of man, of irreligious pride and the waste land it has created, a great affirmation of the power of good. It is indeed, in its yoking of opposites, its depiction of conflict, a metaphysical poem on a grand scale.

The sin of Adam and Eve was the dramatic centre of *Paradise Lost*. *Paradise Regained* (1671) is a simpler kind of drama, in a style of almost uniformly simple statement. Alone in the wilderness, but with light from above, the ideal man, the type of humble obedience, resists all the allurements of the world and, finally, of the intellectual pride that had seduced Eve. It is only with the last temptation and its swift sequel that the hero's divinity is made fully manifest. *Samson Agonistes* (1671) is of course a drama proper, the one classical tragedy in English that stands, in conception and texture, on a level with those of the Greeks. The massive, sinewy verse is still another kind of 'classical' writing, and the movement—notably in the superimposing of one rhythm upon another which G. M. Hopkins called counterpoint—has a new kind of expressiveness. The real drama goes on in the soul of the hero, and there is more than Sophoclean irony and ambiguity, from the title and the first line to the last chorus. Whatever parallels between Samson and himself kindled the poet, eyeless in London under Charles the Second, the result was completely impersonal. Samson, like Christ, resists a series of temptations, but he is a wholly human sinner facing heavier odds, and the process of resistance and regeneration demands the conquest of self and of despair. Further, as Christ's mission was misunderstood by

Mary and the disciples as well as by Satan, so Samson, isolated even from his sympathizers, is alone with God in his inward struggles. Thus in Milton's three major works—not to recall the untried idealism of *Comus*—the theme is temptation; and the old, blind revolutionary, whose public hopes had been crushed, puts his final faith only in God and the individual soul.

CHAPTER III

THE AGE OF REASON AND SENSIBILITY

IF Milton's Christian humanism could accommodate his theological heresies and monistic view of matter and spirit (beliefs which, to be sure, he drew from the Bible), other men would soon go farther, and some had already done so. As Milton and earlier poets had partly seen, the pressure of science and scientific rationalism was radically altering the basis and scope of knowledge and threatening age-old beliefs and values. The great body of encyclopaedic information that had united Aristotle, Pliny, Ptolemy, and Galen with Shakespeare, Donne, and Browne subsided, with relative rapidity, into limbo. Although such leaders of the Royal Society as Boyle and Newton were earnestly religious, the experimental method implied, as always, a complex of forces to be measured rather than a world to be contemplated. Then the traditional conception of nature as the art of God, which could be held by such medical men as Vaughan and Browne, encountered the Hobbesian view of nature, and even of mental experience, as consisting of bodies moving in space and time. Although Hobbes's mechanistic and deterministic materialism was assailed on all sides, it chilled the spiritual and ethical atmosphere— witness the contrast between *Paradise Lost* and Dryden's *The State of Innocence*. Finally, sceptical thought, which had been rising in strength ever since antiquity, brought forth a formidable series of deistic arguments for natural religion as against revelation.

This scientific and critical rationalism, the first conspicuous English phase of the Enlightenment, had obvious effects upon poetry. Much great writing of the age had been born of beliefs, aspirations, and struggles centred in the unquestionable truths of sin, grace, and redemption. Now, for advanced thinkers, God was a theoretical first cause of motion and the world was a mechanical system of bodies of which one contained the aggregates of atoms known as men—a very modern version of the old macrocosm and microcosm which had held God, nature, and man in close association. But if some poets were disturbed, others were not; the veteran Cowley felt no qualms in glorifying not only Dr. Harvey but Hobbes and the bold explorers of the Royal Society. Moreover, if, as Bacon had assumed, truth and reality belonged to science, and poetry to the unreal world of fancy, the inevitable result of the new rationalism was to sap the poet's trust in imagination and intuition, to banish whatever savoured of the irrational, and to encourage direct, verifiable comment upon men and manners, upon unchanged human nature. In other words, men of letters inclined towards a comfortable deism, and poetry became to a large degree public, occasional, mundane, social. Much of it, and much of the best, was satire. We might remember Yeats's remark—perhaps qualifying his censure—that men make rhetoric out of their quarrels with others, poetry out of their quarrels with themselves.

Such an ideological revolution, even if few poets went along with it very far, would affect the language

and tone as well as the motives and themes of
poetry. There was, besides, the concerted effort of
the Royal Society, following Bacon's lead, to establish
a language and style of precise denotation. Neither
the prose of Burton and Milton and Browne nor the
plain prose of more popular writers was a medium
for scientific reports or rigorous thought. And there
was among churchmen—of whom a number had
scientific interests—a parallel reaction against the
purple eloquence of Jeremy Taylor and his kind; one
scientific cleric proposed an act of Parliament 'to
abridge Preachers the use of fulsom and lushious
Metaphors'. The cult of dry, exact, unfigurative
statement in prose helped to remake the canons of
poetry, with some gains no doubt, and certainly
with great losses. It was not Milton and Dryden
but mainly the spirit of science that brought about
'the dissociation of sensibility' (and metaphysical
poetry had gone to seed anyhow). We might describe
a real change in exaggerated form by saying that
whereas the older poets had thought and felt in
images and symbols, the Augustan poets were
inclined to think in prose and add illustrative ornaments.[1]

If in some areas the authority of tradition was
undermined by science, in others it was strengthened
by neo-classicism, and sometimes the two creeds
reinforced each other. It was not until the Augustan
age that neo-classical doctrine was fully formulated—
the *locus classicus* is the young Pope's *Essay on
Criticism*—and commanded the general allegiance of

[1] 'Augustan' refers properly to the Restoration period and
its feeling of kinship with the Rome of Augustus, but it is used
here, as it often is, for the whole age of Dryden and Pope,
roughly 1660–1750.

poets and critics. The key-word is 'nature'—that master-key to a bewildering number of doors in the history of literature and thought. In brief, nature is the rational, civilized, traditional norm in every department of human activity, from metaphysics to etiquette, and literature exhibits both the ideal and departures from it. In poetic practice, since the poet imitates nature, and since the supreme imitators of nature were the ancients, 'To copy nature,' as Pope said, 'is to copy them.' The principle of imitating authors—which was itself ancient—had its good as well as its bad side. It could discourage originality, exalt 'judgment' far above 'wit', and engender academic exercises divorced from life. On the other hand, for good poets, imitation of the ancients meant an active consciousness of the European tradition, of great matter and form and style, of rational and enduring standards of good sense and good taste; on a more practical level, it kept alive the useful distinctness of the various genres and the principles of decorum. If such a creed recoiled from the eccentric, whether in metaphysical conceits or Puritan 'enthusiasm', it was also a civilizing and unifying force; whatever our possible illusions about the cultural solidarity and peace of the Augustans, their standing-ground seemed enviably firm. And the great English exponents of neo-classicism, from Dryden—or Ben Jonson—to Dr. Johnson, had little or nothing of the formalistic rigour of their French counterparts. Even in this one period when neo-classical authority was dominant, English individualism and good sense kept application of 'the rules' within the limits of a healthy flexibility; and other factors contributed to the same result, from

Longinus to Shakespeare and the popular ballads. Dryden, for example, could pronounce Chaucer a more natural, a more truly classical, poet than Ovid.

When we think of the language of Augustan poetry we may think first, perhaps unfairly, of 'poetic diction', of those abstract generalities and inflated periphrases that give a glossy vagueness to so much writing of the period, and not merely of bad poets—the great treasury, if not factory, was Pope's translation of Homer. Such diction, which had begun to appear at the end of the Elizabethan age, came most obviously from the study, writing, and translation of Latin verse; from the uninspired and greatly exaggerated cultivation of one element in Milton; and from the effort both to avoid the 'lowness' of concrete realism (exemplified in Homer and Shakespeare) and to achieve 'the grandeur of generality', an approximation to uniform nature truer than that of particulars. In Milton and earlier writers this poetic diction was not only much more sparing in quantity but was more commonly justified by special purposes; in much Augustan verse it was automatic. The liking for rhetorical periphrasis and generic images was not altogether in harmony with the scientific impulse towards precise denotation, yet the two could flourish together and even support each other, since science itself tends to abstraction and some elements of poetic diction were petrified science.

Augustan prosody could allow of lyrical forms, simple or elaborate, and of miscellaneous measures, notably the tetrameter couplet, and the Miltonic revival stimulated pseudo-Miltonic blank verse, but the main interest centred in the heroic couplet, the closed, balanced, often antithetical pattern that was touched upon in the preceding chapter. Such masters as Dryden and Pope could, like Milton, vary the number and weight of stresses and pauses, and could mix run-on and end-stopped lines and couplets, yet these and other variations, while handled with expressive skill, were confined within relatively narrow limits. We might almost say of the Augustan couplet what has been said of Macaulay's prose style, that it is impossible to tell the truth in it—not that that would have troubled the satirists who used it with such pungent brilliance. The prosodic and other qualities the Augustans admired they traced especially to 'those Standard-bearers of Wit and Judgment, Denham and Waller'. According to Dryden's famous eulogy, the excellence and dignity of rhyme

> 'were never fully known till Mr. Waller taught it; he first made writing easily an art: first showed us to conclude the sense most commonly in distichs, which, in the verse of those before him, runs on for so many lines together, that the reader is out of breath to overtake it. This sweetness of Mr. Waller's lyric poesy was afterwards followed in the epic by Sir John Denham, in his *Cooper's Hill*, a poem which your Lordship knows for the majesty of the style is, and ever will be, the exact standard of good writing.'

The orthodox verdict identified Waller with sweetness and Denham with strength, or, as we might put it, with smooth regularity and conciseness. It is almost an obligation of piety to recall Denham's quatrain on the Thames, which was long admired as the epitome of the virtues it described:

> *O could I flow like thee, and make thy stream*
> *My great example, as it is my theme!*
> *Though deep, yet clear, though gentle, yet not dull,*
> *Strong without rage, without o'erflowing full.*

This kind of writing may not excite us, but the lines do sum up a classical ideal. In general, with regard to matter, style, and versification, we must remember, and respect, what was comprehended in the ideal of 'correctness'. Part of it is contained in 'What oft was thought, but ne'er so well express'd', and the number of semi-proverbial lines from Augustan poets that are lodged in our minds are rough evidence of the finality they could give to the expression of general experience. It was natural that they should especially cherish Horace, the poet of rational moderation, urbanity, and chiselled commonplaces.

We must turn to some poets, or kinds of poetry. The amatory lyrics of the Restoration wits, Rochester, Sedley, Dorset, and others, are the trifles tossed off by gentlemen who wrote with ease, and they seldom rise above a conventional piquancy. A man-about-town polish replaces the delicate art and the idealistic note of the cavalier poets. On that contrast, and the still larger contrast between Restoration and metaphysical poems of love, we may remember Dryden's canonical remark that Donne

'affects the metaphysics, not only in his satires, but in his amorous verses, where nature only should reign; and perplexes the minds of the fair sex with nice speculations of philosophy, when he should engage their hearts, and entertain them with the softnesses of love'.

In the songs in Dryden's plays, nature undoubtedly reigns.

Although the Augustan age did not yield very good or very much lyrical verse, it was, or brought in, the age of hymn-writing; and not many of even the great English lyrics have been so widely known as 'O God, our help in ages past', 'When I survey the wondrous Cross', 'Jesus, lover of my soul', 'O for a closer walk with God', and many others. As poetry the hymns of Isaac Watts, Charles Wesley, and Cowper are not very near the medieval hymns and carols, or the poems of Herbert, but they have the intensity of earnest evangelicalism and are perhaps more moving than the calm deistic assurance of Pope's *Universal Hymn* and Addison's *Ode*.

While the secular lyric rarely soared (and might be represented at its unpretentious best by Prior's *vers de société*), many versifiers, even Watts, joined in what Dr. Johnson called 'the Pindarick folly then prevailing'. We, who have Keats if not Pindar in mind, have difficulty in appreciating even the best of these grandiose, brassy odes. *Alexander's Feast*, the product of Dryden's old age, has certainly strength of a kind, though it seems a libretto less appropriate for Handel than for Sousa. The elegiac ode on Anne Killigrew (1685) is really a celebration of the divine art of poetry (and perhaps the most impressive lines are the not blameless dramatist's rebuke of the licentious stage). This highly organized, highly civilized ode has been regarded as a masterpiece, and yet—despite its larger theme—it suggests a public orator citing a gifted young woman for a celestial degree. It is typical of the age that many beliefs and ideas, while remaining more or less usable, have lost much of their older religious and imaginative actuality and authenticity. At the climactic picture of the day of judgment,

> *When rattling bones together fly*
> *From the four corners of the sky,*

we cannot help remembering

> *At the round earth's imagined corners, blow*
> *Your trumpets, angels, and arise, arise*
> *From death, you numberless infinities*
> *Of souls, and to your scattered bodies go.*

Dryden's use, in his *Song for St. Cecilia's Day*, of traditional ideas of cosmic love and music may also awaken memories of an earlier time, say, of the young Milton's *At a Solemn Music*. As for Pope's ode on St. Cecilia, some passages might have claimed prominence in the author's discourse on the art of sinking.

While our Pindaric pinions are spread, we might fly on a generation to the two mid-century poets especially associated with the ode, Thomas Gray (1716–71) and William Collins (1721–59). Both of course illustrate early phases in the transition from neo-classicism to romanticism. Gray's *Sonnet on the Death of Richard West*—

> *In vain to me the smiling mornings shine,*
> *And reddn'ng Phoebus lifts his golden fire*—

was, we remember, pilloried in Wordsworth's Preface of 1800—though we may remember also that the trite images and language expressed real grief. Gray's early odes were elegant compounds of platitudes, inert conventions, and poetic diction. In the poem on the death of the cat (which becomes a symbol of woman), inflation is adapted to mock-heroic use with humorous irony; but that piece stands apart. No one could have predicted that the author of these things would produce what was to be for many generations, and perhaps still is, the best-known secular poem in the language.

The *Elegy Written in a Country Churchyard* (1751) compelled even Dr. Johnson to put aside his dislike of Gray and 'concur with the common reader': 'The *Churchyard* abounds with images which find a mirror in every mind, and with sentiments to which every bosom returns an echo.' Images and sentiments are general, and poetic diction and abstractions still abound, but if any theme justifies generalities, it is the life and death of the humble and unknown. A scholar-poet's feeling for such people may have been 'pre-romantic', but Gray did not know that; he did know that death, worldly fame, poverty, frustration, and contentment were universal facts and feelings, and the *Elegy* is a mosaic of traditional motifs, classical and modern. The general statements have much Augustan antithesis, and most nouns have their foreordained epithet. Apart from some elaborate periods and inversions, the line or the distich is the unit, and the stanzas are mainly self-contained units (which sometimes could just as well be in a different order); they do, however, have a more contemplative flow than the Augustan couplet allowed. The slow pace and melancholy tone are partly a matter of long vowels and internal

assonance and alliteration. But these things do not
explain why the *Elegy* remains a great poem while its
many congeners are dead. One obvious reason is a
power of style which makes almost every line an
example of 'What oft was thought, but ne'er so well
express'd'. Images, though generalized, can be none
the less evocative. The antitheses are more than
antitheses; they are a succession of dynamic and
ironic contrasts between ways and views of life. And
all this inward force comes from a full sensibility
working under precise control. In its combination
of personal detachment and involvement, as well as
in its generalized texture, the *Elegy* is in some sense
an eighteenth-century *Lycidas*.

In his later Pindaric odes Gray wrote, with energy,
in 'the big bow-wow strain' the genre prescribed,
though his scholarly knowledge or conscience far
excelled his predecessors'. *The Progress of Poesy*, in
title, theme, and substance, may be said to look
backward, while *The Bard* was symptomatic of the
growing interest in medieval and Celtic lore and
bardic poetry (of which Homer was now becoming
the great prototype). Further, in *The Progress of
Poesy* touches of 'wildness' stand out from general
conventionality; in *The Bard*, conventionalities are
included in a general wildness. In the still later
odes, *The Fatal Sisters* and *The Descent of Odin*,
which were free translations, Gray's increasing hold
upon Norse poetry enabled him to escape from
Augustan rhetoric into something like a stark heroic
vein:

> *Now the storm begins to lower*
> *(Haste, the loom of Hell prepare),* . . .

Since Gray had from the first echoed Milton's early poems, it is of interest to find him doing so even in *The Bard* and *The Descent of Odin*.

Although Collins, unlike most of his Latinist predecessors and contemporaries, profited from Greek poetry, he did not bind himself to the Pindaric chariot. He praises the Greek simplicity that fled from Augustan Rome, and at his best he avoids both the turgid and the tepid modes of eighteenth-century verse. If *The Passions* is an exception, its personifications are partly redeemed by lines like these (which, along with other things in Collins, must have been remembered by Keats):

> *They would have thought who heard the Strain,*
> *They saw in Tempe's Vale her native Maids,*
> *Amidst the festal sounding Shades,*
> *To some unwearied Minstrel dancing. . . .*

The titles of most of Collins' odes—*Pity, Fear, Simplicity,* the *Poetical Character, Evening, The Passions, Popular Superstitions of the Highlands*—indicate his prime concern with inward emotion, both normal and 'romantic', rather than with external and public themes. The melodious, unrhymed *To Evening* and 'How sleep the Brave' are lyrical meditations, not orthodox odes. And in creating moods Collins uses particulars as well as generalities; compare, for instance, the third stanza of *To Evening* with the second of Gray's *Elegy*.

While he is most original and attractive in his simpler and quieter pieces, Collins' impassioned imaginative flights show other 'romantic' impulses. It is characteristic, of him at least, that whereas

Gray salutes Shakespeare as 'Nature's Darlιng', the painter of spring and joy (though horror, fear, and tears do squeeze in), Collins invokes him as the supreme poet of fear. Numerous writers, the War-tons and others, were celebrating solitude, revery, enthusiasm (this was now a virtue!), but none of them approached Collins in sensibility and ex-pressive power. In the ode on Highland supersti-tions he leaves not only the city but what was commonly regarded as the country for a world of primitive mystery and terror that stirs and feeds the poetic imagination. Remembering the orthodox Augustan view of 'nature', we appreciate the poet's conscious extension of it to

> scenes like these, which, daring to depart
> From sober truth, are still to nature true. . . .

If in this ode the raw material has not been sufficiently melted down, the same essential spirit is distilled in the *Poetical Character*. Starting from the magic girdle of Spenser's Florimel, Collins revives, with daedal freshness, the traditional idea of the poet as a creator akin to God:

> *The Band, as Fairy Legends say,*
> *Was wove on that creating Day,*
> *When He, who call'd with Thought to Birth*
> *Yon tented Sky, this laughing Earth,*
> *And drest with Springs, and Forests tall,*
> *And pour'd the Main engirting all. . . .*

Here is the renascence of wonder. No other poets of the century have such visions except two who, like Collins, were 'mentally deranged', Christopher

Smart and Blake. In Smart's magnificent canticle, *A Song to David* (1763), enthusiasm and imagination are fused in a religious flame, and—as for Gerard Hopkins—the world is charged with the grandeur of God.

The early eighteenth century yields a quantity of light and humorous verse, from Prior, Gay, and Swift (in his genial moods) up to Goldsmith and Cowper. And there are miscellaneous things of more or less interest, ranging from Lady Winchilsea's 'romantic' musings on nature to Pope's 'romantic' *Eloisa to Abelard*, which made Ovidian rhetoric the medium of religious tension. But the overwhelmingly predominant kinds of verse were the satirical and the reflective, and the best of the former has much more vitality than the best of the latter. Elizabethan satire—including most of Donne's—was the one really dull product of that golden age, but satire was the great channel of Augustan genius. However anti-heroic its method, satire in any age is likely to spring rather from idealism than cynicism, and in Augustan satire perhaps the only real cynic was Rochester. The traditional motive of satire, the chastisement and correction of folly, hypocrisy, and vice, implies a rational and positive and usually conservative standard, and we have observed the central place of reason, nature, and uniformity in the Augustan view of man and society. But however sincerely that ideal, and the didactic motive, were held, we need not discount the satisfaction derived from the exercise of a gift for exposing human weaknesses, especially in individuals one dislikes. Pope was not merely the zealous instructor of mankind when he exultantly proclaimed:

Yes, I am proud; I must be proud to see
Men not afraid of God, afraid of me:
Safe from the Bar, the Pulpit, and the Throne,
Yet touch'd and sham'd by Ridicule alone.

Some men, Samuel Butler and Pope in verse,
Shadwell in a play, and Swift in prose, made fun,
with varying degrees of seriousness, of the pursuits
of the Royal Society and the pretensions of science,
but the main areas of Augustan satire were man and
society, religion and politics, and literature and
writers. Since the classical theory of satire and the
temper of the age set up nature and reason as the
standard of judgment, there might seem to be
discord between the strong Augustan instinct for
generality and satire's essential need of incisive,
arresting particulars (a need that has often led
to a fatal excess of topical detail). Augustan
satirists, like the ancients, did not all follow the
same method.

While we do not read the complimentary odes that
welcomed back Charles II, we do read at least the
first canto of a livelier celebration of Royalist-
Anglican triumph, Butler's *Hudibras* (1663). Compared with later, or with Elizabethan, satires on
Roman models, Butler's portrait of the Puritan
enthusiast, hypocrite, pedant, fool, and knave was
sui generis. The author stood apart from neo-classical
modes in his burlesque use of Don Quixote and
chivalry, his octosyllabic metre, the boisterous high
spirits that gave birth to fantastic rhymes and other
surprises, and the rough but pointed terseness of his
wit. He might almost be said to belong to the
metaphysical line, at any rate the Cleveland branch,

in his linking of dissimilar ideas and images and his
reliance upon a mixture of commonplace and erudite
particulars. But, like the Puritan preachers, Butler
did not know when to stop.

We would give Marvell's satires many times over
for one more lyric (what a change the Restoration
worked in him!), and we would much rather read
Dryden's noble elegy on Oldham than Oldham's
satires on the Jesuits, but *Absalom and Achitophel*
and *MacFlecknoe* (1681-2) are among their versatile
author's chief claims to greatness. In his elaborate
comparison of Horace and Juvenal (*A Discourse
concerning the Original and Progress of Satire*, 1693),
Dryden put Horace first for moral instruction, but
found him less elevated and public-spirited, less
vigorous, sharp, and witty than Juvenal. And yet,
he concluded, however powerful the angry declamation of Juvenal, 'still the nicest and most delicate
touches of satire consist in fine raillery', and that
comes from inborn genius. 'How easy is it', he
observes, 'to call rogue and villain, and that wittily!
But how hard to make a man appear a fool, a block-
head, or a knave, without using any of those oppro-
brious terms!' This is the satirical genius that we
see in Dryden, who preferred to see it in the noble
lord of his dedication. He did, though, cite his own
'character' of Zimri (the Duke of Buckingham),
which gave its original amusement rather than
offence because, instead of railing at crimes, the
satirist touched 'blindsides, and little extravagan-
cies'.

If we do not agree that Zimri is worth the whole
poem, it is only because the other characters and
much of the narrative and speeches manifest such

rhetorical skill, energy, and tartness. One general couplet epitomizes the anti-Puritanism of *Hudibras*:

> *A numerous Host of dreaming Saints succeed,*
> *Of the true old Enthusiastick Breed.*

It is, however, the characters that we come back to—David (King Charles), who so prodigally 'Scatter'd his Maker's Image through the Land'; Achitophel (Shaftesbury), who—like other themes—inspires lines that transcend topical satire:

> *A fiery Soul, which, working out its way,*
> *Fretted the Pigmy Body to decay,*
> *And o'r informed the Tenement of Clay;*

and Shimei (Sheriff Bethel),

> *whose Youth did early Promise bring*
> *Of Zeal to God and Hatred to his King;*
> *Did wisely from Expensive Sins refrain,*
> *And never broke the Sabbath, but for Gain.*

Despite his own comment, Dryden is hardly less good on public than on private faults and vices, and he so merges the individual with the typical that not only the restless, changeable Zimri but the others stand as 'all Mankind's Epitome'. Further, Dryden keeps his temper, no matter how strong his contempt or abhorrence, and his emotional and artistic control intensifies the effect; he displays—to vary Chesterton's phrase about Matthew Arnold's prose—the provoking forbearance of a teacher in an idiot school. When he comes, in the Second Part, to deal with his literary enemies, Settle (Doeg) and especially Shadwell (Og), he is moved to something more than fine raillery—'For ev'ry inch that is not Fool is

Rogue'—but he is most blistering in making the pair absurd. And throughout *MacFlecknoe* (written in 1678), he had wrapped Shadwell in mock-heroic laughter, and literary criticism, rather than abuse. As for the satirist's poetical skill, even our few and brief quotations recall the polished plainness and the suggestive irony of his diction, his variety of movement and tone, and the antithetical shocks so often driven home by forceful rhymes. And even here, as in his more sober poems, Dryden's heroic effects were heightened by imitation of his beloved Virgil.

Satire bulks much larger in the work of Pope (1688–1744) than in Dryden's. There are not only *The Rape of the Lock* (1712–14), *The Dunciad* (1728–43), and the imitations of Horace and Donne (1733–8), but also more or less of the *Essay on Criticism* (1711), *Moral Essays* (1731–5), and *Essay on Man* (1733–4). 'I was not born for Courts or great Affairs', said Pope, in that very witty, sometimes moving, and sometimes disingenuous apologia for a satirist, the *Epistle to Dr. Arbuthnot* (1735), and his satire is chiefly social and literary. He professed, sincerely enough, the orthodox motives; but if his satires were in the tradition of 'delightful teaching', the delight was felt in different ways and degrees by the poet and his few friends who were above reproach, by those victims who could forget their wounds in the enjoyment of others', and by the general literary public. Members of the third class, if they were not 'in the know', would miss a good deal of personal and topical allusion, and modern readers are still farther from coffee-house gossip. Whereas Dryden so generalizes the particular that we get on with a modicum of facts, we must read the *Dunciad* and much else with one eye on footnotes. Of course the special brilliance of Pope's satire depends to a large extent on his pointed particulars—

> *Now Night descending, the proud scene was o'er,*
> *But liv'd, in Settle's numbers, one day more—*

yet he, or the reader, does encounter the law of diminishing returns. At any rate the more we know of classical and later literature the more we enjoy Pope, since he is a very literary poet who gets some of his best results in echoing others.

The *Dunciad* was the offspring of *MacFlecknoe* especially, but, much more than Dryden, Pope 'stinks and stings', or at least stings. In his most comprehensive effort to work off his partly justi-fiable grudges, it is a question if the mock-heroic machinery and the often obscure details are quite witty enough to prevent some tedium—though a number of good critics have no doubts. Whatever may be urged on the ground of Pope's genuine zeal for high standards in literature, the reader may be kept less conscious of positive values than of a great —and successful—artist's pursuit of a shoal of small fry. As for the conclusion, which made the author's voice falter in the reading, and affected Dr. Johnson in the same way, it may seem to us to have more grandiose rhetoric than sublimity.

Pope's 'characters', in the *Epistle to Dr. Arbuthnot* and *Moral Essays*, are partly in line with Dryden's, in that some features belong to human nature in general—

> *Willing to wound, and yet afraid to strike,*
> *Just hint a fault, and hesitate dislike—*

but they may differ in their total effect. Pope is likely to focus his eye so sharply upon his sitters that the typical is more submerged in the individual. And, though he can treat minor victims with something of Dryden's careless contempt, when he wants to draw blood his voice grows shrill. Pope evidently felt a special affinity with Horace, but he seems still more remote from him than from Dryden. The *Imitations of Horace* are commonly read, and well may be, as independent English poems, yet comparison with Horace's satires and epistles enhances our respect for the skilful ease with which Pope transliterates or re-creates the originals in terms of Augustan London. Not that he was much like Horace, except in devotion to his art. Instead of following the ambling pace, the colloquial tone, and the mellow moralizing of Horace, Pope hurries along with a machine-gun in his hands, discharging gibes and aphorisms with equal briskness. However colloquial much of his language and idiom, the steady succession of well-wrought phrases and snapping couplets gives little illusion of casual talk.

The Rape of the Lock is a perfect if not a complete expression of Pope's poetic and satirical genius. It is among other things a classical display of nature and reason as the basis of manners and of departures therefrom as the basis of satire. Both sides in the squabble have been foolish, and their folly is made manifest, but with cool urbanity and grace, since there is nothing here to involve the poet himself and ruffle his temper. (One or two of the dramatis personae were ruffled, and Sir Plume, who inspired one of the most exquisite bits, was moved to threats of violence.)

The mock-heroic scheme, which has a tincture of its opposite, burlesque, was not of course original. The Augustan age had carried on, generally with more crude gusto than art, the comic treatment of classical poems and epic 'machines' which, in England as elsewhere, was a natural reaction from universal veneration, although, as with Boileau and Pope, it did not necessarily imply any lack of real reverence. But Pope went far beyond any predecessor in the polished, pointed refinement and 'deadpan' irony of his epic adaptations, classical and Miltonic, in the complex wit and elegance of his whole conception and texture. And here footnotes are seldom needed, at least if we know the classics; most of the countless particulars are as clear and bright as ever, though they may carry overtones and undertones. It is in such mock-heroic satire, in the witty yoking of opposites, that the Augustans come closest to the metaphysical tradition, though their materials and purposes are so different, and though all things are controlled by a stricter decorum.

In *The Rape of the Lock* strict control rather heightens than diminishes ironical complexity. The world of fashion has a code, shallow and confused though it is, and is shocked by a trifling violation of it. The alternatives of staining 'her Honour, or her new Brocade' belong, by orthodox standards, to very different sets of values, but, in this special world, to the same one. Similar irony envelops husbands and lapdogs and other antithetical conjunctions. As Mr. Tillotson says, the disorder on Belinda's dressing-table—'Puffs, Powders, Patches, Bibles, Billet-doux' —is fundamentally a moral disorder; it carries us back to the sly hints of Herrick's *Delight in Disorder*

and ahead to the dressing-table in *The Waste Land*.
There are contrasts between the natural sun and the
'tinsel Insects' it shines upon, between their irresponsible triviality and the actual world in which
'Wretches hang that Jury-men may dine'. And there
are, at once contrasted with and modified by their
context, gleams of unspoiled nature, of ideal beauty.
To Sir Plume's stuttering expletives the peer replies
with an asseveration that parodies Achilles' oath on
the leafless staff he held, and yet one couplet on the
lock of hair—

> *Which never more its Honours shall renew,*
> *Clipt from the lovely Head where late it grew—*

holds a momentary parallel with FitzGerald's

> *That every Hyacinth the Garden wears*
> *Dropt in her Lap from some once lovely Head.*

Or, if we take a couplet of transparent simplicity,

> *On her white Breast a sparkling Cross she wore,*
> *Which Jews might kiss, and Infidels adore,*

we have a network of paradoxes: the contrast between nature and art (as in Milton and Spenser, but
with a difference); the most sacred and tragic of
religious symbols as the conventional ornament of a
court beauty; the struggle of the Crusaders against
the foes of their faith reduced to the plane of amorous
gallantry; and the conversion of Jews and infidels
into Christians through the power, not of the Cross,
but of the white breast.

If the wit of Pope's more masculine satires is
much less delicate than this, it is still much more

nimble than that of Samuel Johnson's two imitations
of Juvenal, *London* (1738) and *The Vanity of Human
Wishes* (1749). As we might expect from Johnson's
criticism, he refuses to dress his general thoughts
about general nature with the spice of particulars,
and posterity has been fond of deflating

> *Let Observation, with extensive view,*
> *Survey mankind, from China to Peru.*

Yet these serious, sober satires—especially the
second, whose title pretty well sums up Johnson's
sombre outlook—do, with all their abstractions and
monotonous antitheses, leave an impression. Even
generalities can be moving when concentrated phrases
carry the weight of common and painful experience
—'Slow rises worth, by poverty depress'd'; 'Toil,
envy, want, the patron, and the jail'.

The other main body of Augustan verse, after
satire, is the didactic and descriptive, which, like a
wounded snake, or a snake of many segments, drags
its slow length along the pages of the anthologies.
(Dryden's translated *Fables* were uniquely brilliant
examples of narrative, but the modern world seems
to have lost the old taste for mere stories.) The
writing of versified essays and treatises had been
practised extensively by the ancients and revived
during the Renaissance. Of the products of the
Augustan fashion, some are or partake of poetry,
but the majority must be labelled verse (and might
be divided into the flat and the concave). Yet their
prominence and bulk, and the number of their
authors, some of them illustrious, constitute a set
of claims that cannot be entirely ignored; even the
inferior works are a quarry for the historian of ideas,

indeed for any serious student of the period. We can only glance at a representative few. There were two chief categories. One comprised poems of pure argument or reflection, like Dryden's *Religio Laici* (1682) and *The Hind and the Panther* (1687) and Pope's *Essay on Criticism* and *Essay on Man*. The other and looser group includes works that mix, in varying proportions, reflection with natural and topographical description. This line stretches from Denham's *Cooper's Hill* (1642–55) through Pope's *Windsor Forest* (1713), Thomson's *Seasons* (1726–30), and many lesser poems up to (and beyond) *The Traveller* (1764), *The Deserted Village* (1770), and *The Task* (1785). One source of this tradition was Virgil's *Georgics*, though imitators were about as far from him in quality as in time. So strong was the didactic impulse that even Prior responded, with the sceptical and playful *Alma; or, the Progress of the Mind* and the dreary *Solomon on the Vanity of the World*. John Gay, the cheerful extravert who made a delicious opera on the lines of 'a Newgate pastoral', showed originality also in the authentic bucolicism of *The Shepherd's Week* and in his adaptation, in *Trivia*, of the topographical genre to the streets of London.

Dryden has been praised for his skill in conducting an argument in verse, and, though his sobriety is not Lucretian, the praise is deserved, at least for *Religio Laici*. *The Hind and the Panther* has its fine passages, but the whole is long and heavy, and the design was not a happy revival of the old beast-fable. Whatever the connexion of the two works with changing royal policy, they represent stages in the quest of a genuine sceptic; and two lines in the earlier poem foreshadowed his embracing of Catholicism:

Such an Omniscient Church we wish indeed;
'Twere worth Both Testaments, and cast in the Creed.

It is a reminder of the century's preoccupation with the grounds of knowledge and authority, the relations of reason and faith, that *Religio Laici* begins, impressively, with the image that Donne had used in *Biathanatos*: reason is as dim to the soul as the moon and stars, and these grow pale before the sun of supernatural light. In his early *Essay of Dramatic Poesy*, Dryden had rejoiced in the progress of science, which in the preceding hundred years had made greater advances than in 'all those credulous and doting ages' since Aristotle; his poetic defence of Catholicism appeared in the year of Newton's *Principia*.

During this and the next generation there developed, most fully and influentially in Shaftesbury's prose, the doctrines that were more and more to inspire, or dilute, the thought and literature of the age until, along with other impulses, they culminated in the romantic revolt. The age of reason had hardly developed a solid consciousness of being the age of reason when it began to be the age of sentimentalism. Though the new gospel had a Platonic strain, Plato would not have recognized the total result. To oversimplify the matter, we may say that, in opposition to Hobbesian egoism and materialism and scientific rationalism on the one hand, and to irrational Calvinistic pessimism on the other, the new doctrine set up the conception of the natural goodness of man living in responsive harmony with a benevolent universe. Whereas Christian and classical ethics were built on the recognition of a conflict between spirit and flesh, reason and sense, in sentimental ethics the conflict was resolved, or dissolved, through a moral sense that was rather feeling and taste (a mild substitute for the traditional 'right reason'). And whereas for orthodox Augustans the proper study of mankind was man in society, human nature, now external nature acquired new values. Deistic sentimentalism, assimilating Newtonian science, was happy to see in cosmic and terrestrial nature, in the great chain of being, the grand design of the Creator. Thus, though not quite in Browne's sense, nature became again the art of God.

More or less Shaftesburian ideas were basic elements in both the *Essay on Man* and Thomson's *The Seasons*, different as the two works were. Confronted with growing deism, divines had been labouring to make natural religion an ally and not a foe of Christianity, and the public armoury was well equipped with arguments, classical and modern, rational and religious. At such a time, and for such a poet as Pope, the vindication of God's ways to men invited, not a great imaginative work (a 'myth', as we say nowadays), but a persuasive summary of accepted ideas. Pope was perhaps a more logical, and more orthodox, thinker than he has commonly been said to be. Some of his doctrines, like the much-abused 'Whatever is, is right', were, when rightly understood, clearly and essentially Christian. Others, like that of the great chain of being, had long been a part of Christian thought. But what chills the modern reader is not so much Pope's beliefs and ideas in themselves as the way in which they are held and presented. If we set his exposition of order and degree in nature, of the war between good and evil in man, of human pride and ignorance, of the whole human predicament, beside, say, the poems of Davies, Chapman, and Greville (not to mention Spenser, Shakespeare, and Milton), Pope's facile glibness is no less apparent than his verbal brilliance. And both effects are heightened by the metrical movement. The older poets of abstract argument stir our emotions as Pope's bouncing epigrammatic couplets never do. The *Essay* is not a meditation but a declamation.

If Pope was, as Joseph Warton called him, the 'poet of reason', the deism of the young Scot, James Thomson (1700–48), flowed chiefly into the new channel of feeling. And while Pope wrote in his study, Thomson took poetry into an outdoor world that had not been much frequented by Augustan writers, who preferred to keep nature in its place— and its place was seldom in pastorals. Moreover, as his poem on Newton shows in brief, Thomson has, or puts into verse, a more active awareness of science than Pope. Thanks to Newton, he understands as well as admires the rainbow, and he never wearies of extolling the great system of the Newtonian Deity whose hand rolls the planets and stirs every atom, the 'Universal Soul' that 'fills, surrounds, informs, and agitates the whole'. The 'whole' is the great chain of being, which now, in the age of Thomson and Pope, includes sub-microscopic life. But in Pope's static chain of being, any change would be fatal to the ordered scale; Thomson believes in progressive development, up (to quote *The Castle of Indolence* again)

> *from unfeeling mould*
> *To seraphs burning round the Almighty's throne.*

Some such view had been set forth by Milton's Raphael, and it was brought nearer to scientific evolution by Akenside.

It was, though, as a poem of nature that *The Seasons* was long and widely read. In spite of Thomson's generally pedestrian blank verse and pseudo-Miltonic diction, he does really love and observe the manifold and changing phenomena of earth and sky, and along with vague rhapsodizing he has precise description inspired by warm sympathy with man and beast and bird. Like Pope, he has his inconsistencies. He sees nature as beautiful and beneficent, and also as cruel and destructive. He is a primitivist who believes in progress: humanitarian and cultural and commercial progress has been made possible by urban knowledge, though cities are the nurseries of man's vices, and man's natural goodness thrives in the unspoiled ignorance and simplicity of the country. But while Pope's attitude towards the ills of life is one of resigned acceptance, Thomson is in the main on the side of humanitarian effort and benevolent optimism.

When, a generation later, Oliver Goldsmith (1730?-74) perched in the Alps to take a pensive 'prospect of society', he did not share Thomson's and the general faith in British progress and prosperity. A survey of Britain as of other nations drove home the moral that, wherever we may live, 'Our own felicity we make or find'. Though he was allied at some points with the growing humanitarianism of the age, Goldsmith's impersonal moralizing was in much of its substance as conservative as his manner. His didactic generalities were enclosed in regular couplets, and, without being told, we should not be able to guess which eight lines his friend Johnson contributed. Goldsmith's dislike of commercialism was more central in *The Deserted Village*. However nostalgic fancy may have operated, his instinctive sympathy and sentiment—not philosophic sentimentalism—gave the picture a warmth and charm that won it immediate and lasting popularity. In this poem the metrical movement and the manner have exchanged much of their gnomic stiffness and generality for a more natural and varied ease, more concrete detail, and simpler language. Finally, a paragraph on Goldsmith may overlook 'When lovely woman stoops to folly' (which may be known to young readers nowadays chiefly through *The Waste Land*), but not *Retaliation*; the characters of Burke, Garrick, and Reynolds, impromptu sketches in comparison with Dryden's and Pope's engravings, combine insight with good humour.

In the verse of William Cowper (1731–1800)—'a stricken deer, that left the herd'—the instinct for self-expression, and direct expression, is just emerging from the public concerns and manner of neo-classicism. *Boadicea* and 'I am monarch of all I survey' may be called half-romantic. The hymns, if outwardly impersonal, link themselves with such revelations of Cowper's unhappy and despairing self as *The Shrubbery* and *The Castaway*. His translation of Homer, aiming at plainness, achieved a pseudo-Miltonic stiffness, and lacked Pope's energy. The minor didactic poems and the satires retained much of the older style. But when Cowper's amiable psychiatrist, Lady Austen (who had told him of John Gilpin's ride), made the playful suggestion that he write on a sofa, he found happy freedom in interspersing everyday rural scenes with comment on the world. Doubtless in these days *The Task* is read only in samples under academic pressure, but it is an agreeable sedative. Cowper's blank verse and style vary with his topics, and are most attractive on the desultory conversational level. He records, with affectionate intimacy, the familiar ways of nature and man, from the gipsy kettle slung on poles and the lure of hips and haws and bramble-berries to the tea urn, a radish, and an egg by the warm hearth. As a devout Christian, he does not philosophize, like the earlier deists, about benevolent nature and the cosmic design. He respects science, 'baptized' science, but abhors the vain pretensions and measurements of godless research, and the notion of God as a remote First Cause; the 'soul in all things', the 'ceaseless force' that impels all matter, is

> *One Spirit—His*
> *Who wore the platted thorns with bleeding brows.*

And while Cowper is a stout patriot, his humanitarian feelings are outraged by war and negro slavery and men who 'Build factories with blood'.

In general, when we survey the long discursive poem from Dryden to Cowper, we see a movement away from the impersonal treatise towards self-expression, although Cowper would not have thought of this as his aim. It needed a more confidently self-conscious poet to set about a *Prelude*. But we must resist, for the present, the historian's impulse to catalogue the symptoms of romanticism apparent in the eighteenth century. What matters for readers of poetry is the absolute value of the representative body of writing that has just been reviewed; or, since absolutes are out of reach, the value it has for us in the middle of the twentieth century. The nineteenth-century estimate of Dryden, Pope, and the rest was the mainly hostile estimate of the romantic poets, who themselves came in time to embody the ideal of poetry. According to this view, as it was standardized by later critics, the best of the Augustans were the talented versifiers of an age of prose and reason. Modernist criticism, reacting against the romantic tradition and its poetic criteria, has not only canonized the metaphysicals but has rehabilitated Dryden and Pope as great and 'good' artists whose virtues are a rebuke to romantic weaknesses. Such a revaluation has been, up to a point, very wholesome, although we may demur at some excessively zealous claims and assumptions. Without going into these, we might offer some un-fashionable queries or judgments: that the nine-teenth-century estimate holds as much truth as the modern one, if not more; that Dryden and Pope were brilliant artists in satire, but that satire does not rank very high in the poetic scale; that these poets hardly approach the regions where the modern spirit lives; and that the keen pleasure given to a part of our mind by their best work is not at all of the sort that we get from the really great poets, or indeed from many minor ones who have felt the pains and exaltations and mysteries of life.

If these remarks arouse the ire of some readers, let us put Augustan poetry beside that of the sixteenth and the earlier seventeenth century. We need not look at heroic poetry, in which the successors of Spenser and Milton were Blackmore, Glover, and Wilkie—and James Macpherson; nor at lyrical and short poems, of which the Augustan age produced a handful that may be called great, while the earlier period has an almost infinite wealth and variety of great writing. We may grant at once the immense superiority of the Augustans in satire, but with the proviso mentioned above. As for the large division of reflective verse, Dryden and Pope are doubtless finer artists than some of the earlier men, but can they, and others from Thomson to Cowper, be read as —to repeat—we read Daniel, Davies, Chapman, and Greville? The Elizabethans are grappling with problems of culture, knowledge, ethics, religion, that are still our problems, and that are felt in a way we understand and respond to; the problems, or the attitudes, of the later writers are simply dead. All this is not to say that Augustan verse does not contain a good deal of interest in itself and as a partial mirror of an important span in intellectual history; but much of it bears about the same relation to poetry that the period's family groups on canvas bear to great painting.

Incidentally, although the clarity of general truth was a conscious aim of the eighteenth-century writers, the extreme obviousness of their reflective and most other verse suggests some decline in the mental equipment of readers if not of poets. When we think of both the knowledge and the intelligence that the older poets in general assumed, must we invoke that good old standby, the rise of the middle class, as an explanation of the lower level of cultivation and acuteness and sensitivity?

CHAPTER IV

ROMANTICISM

THE artistic and philosophical tenets of neo-classicism can be completely summarized, as indeed they were by Pope, and can be readily applied, notwithstanding qualifications and exceptions, to Augustan poetry. But what common denominator links together, as 'romantic', Burns, Blake, Coleridge, Wordsworth, Scott, Landor, Byron, Shelley, Keats, and such lesser poets as Southey, John Clare, Leigh Hunt, and that isolated realist of rural life, George Crabbe? The label—which, like 'metaphysical', was not used by the poets themselves—means so many things that it may seem at first to have no meaning at all. And the fullest statement of the romantic creed, *Biographia Literaria* (1817), though parts of it are alive in the critical theory of our time, has, in comparison with Pope's *Essay on Criticism*, a limited and erratic helpfulness for the understanding of the romantic poets; it is infinitely suggestive on some central matters and slights others. But, if we put along with it Keats's letters, Wordsworth's Preface to the second edition (1800) of *Lyrical Ballads*, and Shelley's *Defence of Poetry*, and add Hazlitt's *Lectures on the English Poets*, we do find the common denominator of the greatest poets, that is, a new and intense faith in the imagination.

Besides the abundance and variety of genius, there are other reasons for the complexity of romanticism. In the Augustan age poets, critics, and literary public were united in relative harmony of judgment, and the general view of the contemporary poetical hierarchy was much the same as ours. But in the romantic age there were marked divisions of taste and outlook among poets, critics, and readers. The poets whom we think of as dominating the scene were a small, loose group of *avant-garde* writers who had small, if growing, audiences. Blake, whom nowadays some worshippers would place on the throne, was ignored even by most of his fellow poets—though we may remember Crabb Robinson's remark, 'There is no doubt this poor man was mad, but there is something in the madness of this man which interests me more than the sanity of Lord Byron or Walter Scott!' The briefest and best picture of the general cleavage comes from Byron, the self-conscious patrician who shared the conservative taste of gentlemen. As late as 1819, speaking in scorn of 'the Lakers', and summing up both critical and popular orthodoxy, Byron said:

> *Scott, Rogers, Campbell, Moore, and Crabbe, will try*
> *'Gainst you the question with posterity.*

Posterity did decide the question within a few decades, although in 1879 Matthew Arnold, in his essay on Wordsworth, could still, perhaps in partial deference to tradition, count not only Scott but Campbell and Moore among 'our chief poetical names' (in a list of seventeen that did not include Marlowe, any of the metaphysicals, or Blake).

We talk, rightly enough, about the romantic revolt, but we recognize that the movement had been growing throughout the 'age of reason' and that it was a natural culmination of complex and converging impulses. What in the first years of the eighteenth century had been a rivulet of sentimentalism became in Wordsworth a deep stream, in Blake a foaming flood. And, just as English neo-classicism had been more moderate and flexible than that of the Continent, so English romanticism (apart from Blake) was more moderate and flexible than its continental counterpart. The neo-classical age had been one of formal schooling in the virtues of intelligence, and it had achieved those virtues in a degree that made the best Augustan poetry unique in English literature. But the finest spirits of a later age were less conscious of the achievement—by which they profited—than of the cost, and a more accurate if more cumbrous label for romanticism would be 'the anti-rationalist movement'. The revolt against reason, or against the actual or supposed eighteenth-century conception of it, comprehended everything from a revulsion against a mechanized universe and a mechanized psychology to a revulsion against the Augustan heroic couplet, which (as in Keats's outburst in *Sleep and Poetry*) had a mechanistic significance too.

The many related symptoms are familiar: the turning from reason to the senses, feelings, imagination, and intuition; from the civilized, modern, and sophisticated to the primitive, medieval, and natural; from urban society to rural solitude; from preoccupation with human nature to preoccupation with the aesthetic and spiritual values of external nature; from mundane actuality to visions of the mysterious, the ideal, and the infinite; from satire to myth; from the expression of accepted moral truth to discovery of the beauty that is truth; from realistic recognition of things as they are to faith in progress; from belief in God and evil to belief in man and goodness; from established religious and philosophical creeds to individual speculations and revelations; from normal, generic abstractions to the variety of concrete particulars; from impersonal objectivity to subjectivism; from public to private themes; from formal correctness to individual expressiveness; from the ideal of order to the ideal of intensity; from the poetry of prose statement to image and symbol; from poetic diction to common language; from self-conscious traditionalism to self-conscious originality; from the rational sobriety of Latin literature to romantic Hellenism. . . . It is needless to add that these brief headings need to be qualified in both directions, and to repeat that these impulses had been more or less visible from the early eighteenth century onwards, and that they appear in the romantic poets in partial and variable permutations and combinations.

Yet however we qualify such a catalogue, it does constitute a revolutionary change, not only in the view of the character and function of poetry but in the whole conception of the nature of man and of the world in which he finds himself. One large implication, which has grown more conspicuous in our time, is the estrangement of the poet, the artist, from society. No doubt some such separation has existed ever since the first bard sang and the first audience grunted, but we think of poets before the romantic age—Chaucer, Spenser, Shakespeare, Milton, Dryden, Pope—as ordinary citizens, sharing the experience and general outlook of the educated community. And poets as a rule, at least up through Milton, were

not merely writers but were more or less involved
with everyday occupations. Most of the chief
romantic poets had no such employment in the
workaday world; and whatever their interest in
public affairs, they were spectators on the sidelines.

Other circumstances contributed to set them apart
from the mass of men. They conceived of the poet
as not merely a man of literary talent describing and
assessing life about him but as a prophet and oracle,
a pilgrim of eternity and infinity (so, to be sure, had
Milton thought of himself, but he was a Christian and
a citizen first and a poet second). Yet, along with a
conception of the poet even more exalted than that
of the Renaissance, went a consciousness that mankind was now too much engrossed in getting and
spending to feel the need of poetic illumination. The
industrial revolution was inaugurating what was to
make the greatest change in human life since history
began, and it was founded on ideas and values
altogether alien from those of the artist. The romantic poets saw developing around them a general
worship of machinery and Mammon, the imprison-
ment and corruption of the natural man. And while
poets sympathized, for a time, with the French
Revolution, or at least cherished hopes of progress,
the mass of their countrymen were frightened into
reactionary suppression of liberty. A still more
significant fact, perhaps, is that, for the first time in
English history, the leading poets stood outside
established religious creeds and sought a working
faith of their own—though Coleridge and Wordsworth eventually turned to orthodoxy and others
have been called *animae naturaliter Christianae*.
Finally, as we observed at the start, the new poetry

seemed, to conservative taste, strange and wild and
odd, and it made its way slowly. Thus for many
reasons, whether accidental or essential, romantic
poetry was at first less representative of the general
taste and outlook than the products of Augustan
coteries had been. All these remarks must again be
qualified; but in surveying the poets of any earlier
age one would not be led to make them at all.

Romantic poetry does not, like that of the Augustans, fall into two or three large divisions, and we
have to choose between giving thumb-nail sketches
of eight or nine poets and slicing them up under
some of the numerous general headings listed a few
pages back. Possibly the first will be the lesser evil,
if not done in entire forgetfulness of the second; and
we may begin with three poets who, in different
ways, stand relatively apart from the rest.

Allowing for the many 'pre-romantic' manifesta-
tions, from Collins—or Pope—to Chatterton and
Cowper, we commonly date the romantic revolt from
Lyrical Ballads (1798). But the earliest and by far
the most revolutionary rebel, and the most difficult
poet, was William Blake (1757–1827). His lyrical
volumes were *Poetical Sketches* (1783), *Songs of
Innocence* (1789), and *Songs of Experience* (1794);
between the last two came *The Marriage of Heaven
and Hell* and the first prophetic books. The youthful
Poetical Sketches contained both poetical diction—
such as 'Phoebus fir'd my vocal rage'—and reminis-
cences of Elizabethan and early seventeenth-century
song. 'My silks and fine array' is always cited, and it
does sound a strange note in 1783, though it could
hardly be mistaken for an Elizabethan lyric.
'Memory, hither come' and the *Mad Song* have

echoes of Milton and Shakespeare but are not Miltonic or Shakespearian. In general even the immature singer of pastoral joy reveals a new sensibility and manner. *To the Evening Star*, with the hovering movement of its unrhymed verse and such phrases as 'wash the dusk with silver', makes Collins' ode seem a little stiff and literary.

But Blake's lyrical development owed less to the older English poetry than to Isaac Watts's poems of childhood, and *Songs of Innocence* carried his own peculiar blend of the earthly and unearthly. The first stanza of the first poem has a lilt and an imaginative *naïveté* that belong to no one else:

> *Piping down the valleys wild,*
> *Piping songs of pleasant glee,*
> *On a cloud I saw a child,*
> *And he laughing said to me. . . .*

It is Blake's lyrics—including the late and famous 'And did those feet in ancient time'—that most completely fulfil the definition of romanticism as 'the renascence of wonder'. The world of nature and man is the world of love and beauty and innocence enjoyed by a happy child, or rather by a poet who miraculously retains an unspoiled and inspired vision. But in *Songs of Experience* the serpent has corrupted Eden, and themes that before had the radiance of spontaneous purity and joy are darkened by a knowledge of age and evil and suffering and oppressive authority. The most striking if not the most typical contrast is that between *The Lamb* and *The Tiger*, between a primitive painting of the innocent child, lamb, and Christ, and a fiery incantation, a symbolic hymn of wonder and terror and power. In the only earlier poem that can be linked with *The Tiger*, Smart's *Song to David*, the ecstatic catalogue of the lion's strength and all the other glories of creation culminates in Christ's redeeming sacrifice; Blake is celebrating the untamed forces in man and nature that must shatter unnatural ethical restraints and mechanistic philosophies.

The paradoxical statement of Blake's creed, *The Marriage of Heaven and Hell*, does much to explain the symbolism of *The Tiger* and the main themes of the voluminous prophetic poems. The Bible and sacred codes have divided man into body and soul, have associated the body with energy and evil and the soul with reason and good, and have proclaimed eternal torment for him who follows his energies. The contrary is the truth. The body is not distinct from the soul (so, by the way, Milton had said, though he did not go on to Blake's conclusions); the body 'is a portion of Soul discern'd by the five Senses, the chief inlets of Soul in this age'; and 'Energy is the only life', is 'Eternal Delight'. 'The road of excess leads to the palace of wisdom.' 'The roaring of lions, the howling of wolves, the raging of the stormy sea, and the destructive sword are portions of eternity too great for the eye of man.' 'The tigers of wrath are wiser than the horses of instruction.' 'Sooner murder an infant in its cradle than nurse unacted desires.' Whatever the varied sources of Blake's thought and feeling, his doctrines are obviously the climactic explosion of eighteenth-century senti-mentalism, the faith in the spontaneous goodness of man; and, no less obviously, they are in the tradition of older and later naturalism. The scientific, logical reason and traditional ethics are anathema, and particular and recurrent objects of denunciation are Newton and Locke and Bacon, who stand for the effort to confine cosmic and human energies within mechanical rules. Two generations earlier, at a time when science and poetry seemed to be in accord, James Thomson had linked these and other scientific thinkers with Chaucer, Spenser, Shakespeare, and Milton; Blake sets Milton and Shakespeare and Chaucer in opposition to his evil trinity. 'Art is the Tree of Life ... Science is the Tree of Death.' In place of rationalistic and repressive creeds and codes, Blake exalts imagination, energy, love, as the divine inward guides. The poet is the only true man, and every man is a poet, or would be if his vitality and creative power had not been cramped and deadened by civilization, conventional religion, and science; he must burst his mind-forged manacles and fulfil his potentialities. Great rebels against artificial authority are Christ and Milton; it is difficult to recognize either in what are really Blake's projections of himself.

The gospel is set forth in the huge prophetic books, in terms of a complex and occult mythology, and these poems are labyrinths that only devotees penetrate. Blake has had many learned, acute, and devout expositors in modern times, and he seems to be commonly regarded as a supreme poet and myth-maker and as more Christian than Christians. That may be so. But the ordinary reader may possibly find the non-lyrical poet's symbolism baffling and his prophetic doctrine the great modern expression of a naturalistic, undiscriminating worship of 'Life'. At any rate, though the power of his message is muffled by his esoteric manner, Blake appears among the romantic poets like a force of nature among men writing with pen and ink.

It is an abrupt reminder of the comprehensiveness of romanticism to turn from Blake to the least complex and philosophic of the major figures, Burns and Scott. Robert Burns (1759–96) won immediate fame with his first Scottish poems (1786), partly because of the freshness and tang of their substance and dialect, partly because he looked like the great fulfilment of the eighteenth-century quest of a primitive poet. And the author of the *Epistle to J. Lapraik*, who preferred 'ae spark o' Nature's fire' to book-learning, might have seemed to be accepting that role. In fact, of course, the 'Heaven-taught ploughman' was quite well-read in the chief English poets and especially in eighteenth-century literature (even that incomparable dramatic monologue, *Holy Willie's Prayer*, has an epigraph from Pope); and he was misled into writing some insipid English verse. Burns was a warm admirer of Henry Mackenzie's *Man of Feeling*, and *The Cotter's Saturday Night* and *To a Mountain Daisy* mix authentic inspiration with the convention of sensibility. But Burns was also an avowed disciple of the less genteel Robert Fergusson and Allan Ramsay, he was steeped in the whole Scottish tradition from the Chaucerians downward, and he recognized the nature of his own gifts. After the Kilmarnock volume (enlarged in 1787) came *Tam O'Shanter*, that swift masterpiece of the comic supernatural which is equally far from Sir Calidore's vision of the Graces and from *Peter Bell*, and the large and varied body of songs, re-created and original, on which Burns spent his later years. In these he struck again the simple notes of love that had not been heard for generations, and of pathos that had scarcely been heard at all; the bawdy had an unbroken tradition.

We may link Burns historically with the romantic movement by virtue of his lyrical genius, his poetical debt to popular song and folk-lore, his instinctive use of concrete particulars and images, the sharply picturesque energy of his homely language, and his republican and equalitarian sentiments and sympathetic kinship with the lowly, the erring, and the outcast. But such phrases only begin to explain why Burns has had such a peculiar attraction for the plain man who 'doesn't read poetry', and why Burns Societies have been so different from Browning Societies. One uses the past tense, uncertainly and regretfully, because of late—outside Scottish circles—Burns seems to have fallen into neglect. He has been almost entirely ignored by the intellectual critics of our day, since a prolonged hold upon the affections of the mass of men is distasteful to the sophisticated mind. Our somewhat wire-drawn critical dogmas are not receptive towards either simple songs, or, say, such a primitive, unabashed, and, in its squalid way, heroic carnival of anarchic individualism as *The Jolly Beggars*—a work extolled by the fastidious Arnold. Besides, as with Henryson and Dunbar, the language which is so extraordinarily alive is also a practical barrier. But, for those who can surmount the glossary, there is a great lyrist, humorist, and satirist, whose warm humanity, spiced by an aversion to 'the unco guid', is irresistible.

Sir Walter Scott (1771–1832) perhaps lacked, even more than his predecessor, conscious 'ideas' that

belong to the romantic movement (though his total
influence upon ideas was immense). But if Scott was
feudal rather than republican, and cared nothing for
doctrines of universal brotherhood, he was in fact
every man's brother. The closest affinity between
Scott and Burns is in the utter reality, comic or
serious, of the lower-class and 'Robin Hood' characters of the Scottish novels and the metaphorical
raciness of their speech. There was affinity also in
their devotion and debt to Scottish songs and ballads,
and Burns's work had its complement in *Minstrelsy
of the Scottish Border* (1802–3). After a flirtation with
German romanticism, Scott came back to his true
love, and it was the Scottish ballads that made him a
poet, for a poet, at times, he was. Modern scholar-
ship would shudder at the merging and revising of
variant versions, but Scott was nearer to Bishop
Percy than to Professor Child, and, like Burns, he
could enter, indeed could not help entering, into
the spirit of his originals. Thus he could re-create
Kinmont Willie and create Elspeth's tale of 'the red
Harlaw' or the purely lyrical *Proud Maisie*. Scott's
ballads and songs are, as we might expect, more
martial and, in the common meaning of the word,
romantic than Burns's; the two might be said to
divide between them the themes Wordsworth imagined for his solitary reaper.

Scott's once very popular romances of the Scottish
past, *The Lay of the Last Minstrel* (1805) and the rest,
which he enjoyed writing but did not take very seri-
ously, are doubtless not much read in our century
(juvenile readers now seem to begin with Donne and
Hopkins). But if they are romantic hokum, they are
hokum of the best quality, the work of a minstrel

who had a spark of Homer in him—if not the full
flame that Thomas Hardy saw.

Burns and Scott had, or found, a more living
popular tradition behind and around them than was
immediately available to their English contemporaries. But Wordsworth (1770–1850) and Coleridge
(1772–1834), needing to escape from effete convention and get a fresh start, went back also to the
ballads—not always to pure or authentic specimens
—as well as to the great English poets. They began
in orthodox fashion, but discovered their true vein,
of course, in the volume that bore the significant
title *Lyrical Ballads*. The poetic wedding of Coleridge
and Wordsworth was a quieter affair than *The
Marriage of Heaven and Hell*. Yet the world of the
Lyrical Ballads was a world of blended innocence and
experience. It was decided, as we all know (from the
fourteenth chapter of *Biographia Literaria*), that
Wordsworth should present everyday characters and
incidents in the revealing light of imagination, and
that Coleridge was to give 'supernatural, or at least
romantic' characters 'a human interest and a sem-
blance of truth sufficient to procure for these shadows
of imagination that willing suspension of disbelief
for the moment, which constitutes poetic faith'.
Wordsworth's share might, in theory, have been
sanctioned by Dr. Johnson's definition: 'Poetry is
the art of uniting pleasure with truth, by calling
imagination to the help of reason'; Coleridge's would
fall under the censure, in *Rasselas*, of 'the dangerous
prevalence of imagination'. In some of Wordsworth's contributions the light of imagination was
not kindled. But the child of *We Are Seven*, who
cannot feel the actuality of death, inhabits a corner

of Blake's world. And in the poems on 'Lucy Gray' in the second edition, ballad-like simplicity ranges from the thin pathos of the story of her death to the lyrical sublimity of *A Slumber Did My Spirit Seal*. Such intimations of immortality are a long way from the popular ballads.

The Rime of the Ancient Mariner, for all its use of the traditional devices, is no less remote from the archetypes. To keep to the simplest terms of a theme that has multiple and tantalizing layers of meaning, the Mariner commits a sin that isolates him from his kind and that is partly expiated when his heart is filled with love of God's creatures and he is restored to harmony with nature, though he remains a ghostly wanderer. As for the material, *The Road to Xanadu* has shown how the most widely scattered details, from books of travel and science and poetry, were woven into a unified whole. The extraordinary vividness and brevity of the concrete images comes partly from Coleridge's power of phrase, partly from his 'naïve' approach. As in folk-tales and dreams, the preternatural and supernatural are not built up by a sceptical poet for a sceptical audience but are rather assumed as natural or at least possible. In *Christabel*, on the other hand, to move beyond *Lyrical Ballads*, the atmosphere owes much to the stock properties of Gothic romance (and of course to the rhythm), so that the effect, though still potent, is rather a construction than an unquestioned reality; and the juxtaposition of innocence and evil lacks something of the mythic quality of the *Ancient Mariner*. In *Kubla Khan* 'the dangerous prevalence of imagination' reaches its apogee; the poet surrenders to an intoxicating vision of poetic inspiration.

The popular ballads had been increasingly read since the time of Addison, and many Augustan writers had composed elegant or humorous imitations, but their real power did not work until it led Coleridge and Wordsworth to write poems at once so different from each other's and from the originals. Both poets found in the ballads poems of imagination untrammelled by the artificialities of civilized life, and models of direct simplicity in language and tone. Wordsworth, dealing with homely modern incidents, used homely modern language (with the influence of the ballads may be linked that of Burns); Coleridge, in keeping with his weird tale, drew a good deal upon archaism, though that was modified in revision.

The theory of poetic language enunciated in Wordsworth's Preface of 1800 was, as a manifesto against eighteenth-century poetic diction and a justification of a return to natural speech, essentially sound, though the author somewhat overstated it and left himself open to Coleridge's later criticism of both his theory and his practice. In his best poems, and especially in his longer ones, Wordsworth did not stick even to 'a selection' of the language actually used by men; yet he did virtually destroy lifeless language and give poetry a medium of fresh and natural vitality. Wordsworth stresses the speech of country people because it has suffered less from the deadening uniformity and restraints of sophisticated intercourse and is the direct expression of feeling. Thus for him, as for the Augustans, 'nature' is a norm, though on a different level.

More important still is the setting up, or rather the restoring, of something like the traditional conception of the high responsibility and wide range of poetry. The kind of pleasure the poet gives is especially needed in an age of external excitements and inward torpor that craves gross and violent stimulants. The poet, 'a man speaking to men', can share his own sensitive and abundant life with others. Poetry is not an extraneous ornament; it is both 'the spontaneous overflow of powerful feelings' and 'the breath and finer spirit of all knowledge'. And Wordsworth is so confident of the all-embracing and quickening power of poetry that he can see it attending the discoveries of science as these become absorbed into human experience. He did recoil from the human or inhuman consequences of the industrial—that is, the scientific—revolution, but he could not foresee the plight of the modern poet, whom scientific positivism has left to the contemplation of a great void. Moreover, when we put Wordsworth's ideal of the poet-teacher beside that of Spenser and Milton, it is clear that he does not stand on the once firm rock of the Christian-classical tradition. His standing ground, like the modern's, is what the poet can establish for himself, although, unlike the modern, Wordsworth has few qualms.

The Wordsworth of the Preface was riding on an even keel, but he had been storm-tossed in earlier years. The circumstances of his youth and his temperament had made him an instinctive radical to whom the French Revolution was a no less natural than welcome event, and whose sympathy isolated him from his fellow-countrymen. When Revolutionary zeal became aggressive imperialism, what had been his great prop was knocked from under him.

Seeking something positive to believe in, he turned
to thinkers like William Godwin, whose cool analytical reason seemed to promise the millennium. But
doctrinaire rationalism, built on the conception of
man as a head without a heart or senses, gave only
dusty answers, and Wordsworth 'Yielded up moral
questions in despair'. Finally, with the aid of his
sister Dorothy—'She gave me eyes, she gave me ears'
—and of Coleridge, he returned, with a new need and
understanding, to his first love, nature, the world
of the senses and feelings and imagination that never
betrayed her votaries. And, while still an obscure
young poet of twenty-eight, Wordsworth was so
convinced of the significance of his process of salvation that he launched upon the vast poem, *The
Recluse*, which was to record his experience and
philosophy in full. Of this work he wrote large
portions, the personal and preparatory *Prelude* and
The Excursion (1795–1814), and a first book of which
the noble conclusion was printed as a 'Prospectus'
with *The Excursion*. It was typical of romantic
self-consciousness that the heroic poem of antiquity
and the Renaissance should have turned into a
poet's spiritual autobiography. The first version of
The Prelude (1798–1805) was somewhat altered,
especially in the direction of orthodox Christianity,
before it was published in 1850. It would be hope-
less to attempt here any formal comment on
Wordsworth's grand testament, though scarcely any
observation can be made about him that is not
partly based on it. That is not to say that the poem
is all poetry.

About the time he began *The Prelude*, Wordsworth gave a brief account of his development in

Tintern Abbey, his main contribution to *Lyrical Ballads*. The poem was, among other things, the intensely personal culmination of the eighteenth-century topographical-reflective genre. It was also the finest poem in blank verse that had been written since Milton; Wordsworth's power and purity of expression are such that we are almost unconscious of the beautiful medium and share his experience directly. He saw his association with nature as having had three stages. First there had been the animal activity of a boy at large among hills and woods and streams; with adolescence had come a wholly aesthetic passion for the beauty and mystery of nature; and finally, as the capacity for sensuous ecstasy faded, feeling for nature was more and more bound up with 'the still, sad music of humanity' and with the consciousness of a spirit animating and uniting all things, sky and ocean and green earth and the mind of man. Whatever these three stages owed to David Hartley's associationist psychology, and however retrospection, here or in *The Prelude*, may have modified literal fact, the pattern of development was Wordsworth's most precious possession and assurance.

Coleridge also had had millennial dreams, revolutionary and Pantisocratic, and, through disillusionments and vicissitudes, had arrived at a similar faith in a divine spirit pervading all things and linking nature with man. That is the philosophic and religious theme of the series of reflective poems, *This Lime-Tree Bower My Prison, Frost at Midnight, Fears in Solitude*, and others. Both poets were reacting against the scientific, rationalistic, and mechanistic view of nature and man, and their positive faith contained elements of eighteenth-century sentimentalism and seventeenth-century Platonism. The poetic imagination transcends mere intellect; it is 'reason' in its highest and purest form, the intuitive faculty by which man apprehends unity and reality.

In the spring of 1802 the two poets were together, Wordsworth happily active, Coleridge weighed down by physical and mental distresses. Now, four years after *Tintern Abbey*, when moments of sensory vision were still fewer and dimmer, Wordsworth took up again the theme of the earlier poem. *Intimations of Immortality* was, except in its irregular lines, very different from Augustan Pindarics (Wordsworth had, by the way, just been reading Ben Jonson, and he may have had in mind the rhythms of Jonson's ode on Cary and Morison). He began with a lament for his loss of sensuous experience, a loss that seemed to leave him a dead thing in a world of life and beauty; but, as in *Tintern Abbey*—with the added and not wholly happy 'Platonic' theme—he went on to recognize the compensation age had brought, his growth in maturity and humanity, his deeper understanding of man's joys and sorrows and of the oneness of man and nature. Coleridge, hearing the first part of the uncompleted poem, wrote his melancholy reply, *Dejection*. He has lost his shaping spirit of imagination, which alone gives life to nature, without which the world is a flat and joyless scene; and he has found no compensation.

The young Pope had imbibed from William Walsh the ideal of 'correctness', which English poets had seldom regarded; Wordsworth, when he was about fourteen, set before himself the depiction of 'the infinite variety of natural appearances which had

been unnoticed by the poets of any age or country',
so far as he knew. The result was, of course, one of
Wordswórth's chief historical claims to greatness, that
he did, in an iron time, re-create the life of nature
and the human senses. In fact, however, his poetry
contains much less precise observation than we
might have expected, and much less than the
'peasant poet' John Clare affords (though Clare
became more than a loving observer); Wordsworth
had less interest in natural phenomena than in his
own spiritual reactions, conscious and unconscious.
And his disillusionment with rationalistic thought,
which found vent in anti-bookish and anti-intellectual
outbursts, intensified his trust in nature's healing
power. Having no positive Christian belief, he could
satisfy his idealistic soul only by making nature
supernatural.

But though it is customary to see much of Wordsworth's finest writing in his poems of wise passiveness
and joy, it may be doubted—in spite of centenary
essays of 1950—if the modern reader can bring a
willing suspension of disbelief to the poet's animistic
view of nature or is captured by the smaller voice of
Wordsworth the bird-watcher. Granting his great
historical significance as the poet of nature and the
senses, we may think that he lives chiefly as the poet
of 'man, the heart of man, and human life', whether
in the 'Lucy' poems and *The Solitary Reaper* or
Michael or parts of *The Prelude* and *The Excursion*.
He was, to be sure, rather a lover of man than of
men (and above all, an observer of himself), and his
deserted women, shepherds, beggars, and leech-
gatherers are not so much persons as humble examples
of pathos and fortitude. And though in general

Wordsworth's utterance may be consummate in expressions of his 'magical view' of nature, and may decline when that is exchanged for a stoic view of human life, we may think that the poetry of simple joy is rather too simple in comparison with the poetry of partial doubt and conflict. Wordsworth began, quite early in 'the great decade', to discover that neither external nature nor inward spontaneity of impulse was an adequate support against the ills of life and death or an adequate moral guide. Many readers resent the *Ode to Duty*, the *Character of the Happy Warrior*, and *Laodamia*, but they would at least admit that there is poetry in *Resolution and Independence*, the sonnets of 1802 and a number of later ones, the *Elegiac Stanzas*, and even at times in *The Excursion*. And if Wordsworth's growth in wisdom is to be related to his loss of poetic power, in what way are these poems more overtly didactic, more composed of plain moral statement, than *Lines Written in Early Spring*, *Expostulation and Reply*, *The Tables Turned*, *To My Sister*, and other early expressions of the gospel of nature, including *Tintern Abbey* itself?

If we take Wordsworth (allowing for what he absorbed from Coleridge) as the most germinal influence in English romanticism, his nearest heir and affinity, in some matters of thought and feeling rather than style, was John Keats (1795–1821). We must add, of course, that their poetry was very unlike; that Keats felt many influences, from the Elizabethans to Leigh Hunt and Hazlitt; and that, in the short process of his growth, he became himself a master and probably the chief romantic influence on the poetry of the century. Yet his response to

Wordsworth leads us into the centre of some of his main problems.

Keats's attack on Augustan verse in *Sleep and Poetry* (1816)[1] carried echoes of Wordsworth and of Hazlitt. In the same poem the young poet's view of his present und future recalls the stages of Wordsworth's development outlined in *Tintern Abbey*, but with characteristic differences. The rock and cataract of Wordsworth's adolescent passion become the realm of Flora and old Pan; and, while Wordsworth had already arrived at his third stage, of human sympathy, the young Keats must drive himself to contemplate leaving the sensuous luxuries of nature for 'the agonies, the strife Of human hearts'. A similar sequence is elaborated in the letter (3 May 1818) on the mansions of life and poetry, where *Tintern Abbey* is cited. And in many letters Keats reveres or recoils from the older poet. Shakespeare, the dramatic creator who has no philosophical axe to grind, is the supreme example of 'negative capability', and Keats would have him as his tutelary genius. But he is also powerfully drawn to Milton and Wordsworth; while Milton is the finer artist, Wordsworth, because of the general progress of thought, has seen further into the human heart, into common and tragic experience. On the other hand, Keats dislikes the Tory egotist that Wordsworth has become and at times even his poetry, which has a palpable design upon us. Thus his vacillation between Milton and Wordsworth is roughly a vacillation between concern with the art of poetry and concern with its spiritual value.

[1] Dates attached to the poems of Keats and Shelley are dates of composition, not of publication.

Wordsworth is more or less involved in related problems. Must the poet possess formal knowledge and logical reason, or should he rely on his imagination and intuition for the kind of knowledge that eases 'the burthen of the mystery'? Keats can shift from one principle to the other, though the second is predominant. If the much-quoted 'O for a Life of Sensations rather than of Thoughts' is not simply, as Mr. Garrod translates it, 'O for the pure gospel of the *Lyrical Ballads*', it is a plea for the intuitive life of the artist. In the same letter (22 November 1817), written when *Endymion* is finished, Keats gives his first clear statement on life and poetry, a very strong and comprehensive statement that links itself with Hazlitt's first lecture on the English poets and—though Keats does not know it—with Blake:

'I am certain of nothing but of the holiness of the Heart's affections and the truth of Imagination—What the Imagination seizes as Beauty must be truth—whether it existed before or not—for I have the same Idea of all our Passions as of Love, they are all in their sublime, creative of essential Beauty.'

Yet the proclaimer of such a creed can be afflicted, most acutely in his last long poem, *The Fall of Hyperion*, by the question whether poetry is a justifiable activity, where it stands in comparison with simple goodness and humanitarian action. And what of the ideal artist who has no moral identity when man needs painful experience to achieve identity and become a soul? It is the complexity of Keats's Apollonian and Faustian tensions and the

depth of his aesthetic and ethical insights that make
him the most modern of the romantic poets, the one
who speaks to us most directly. But we must ask
how far the wisdom of the man and the letter-writer
got into his poetry.

We may notice first several poems that are relatively lacking in 'ideas'. *Isabella* (1818), though it has
some fine bits, is as a whole a tissue of romantic
pathos that has deserved its popularity with school-
girls. *The Eve of St. Agnes* (1819), the work of a
happy lover, is incomparably better, so rich in
pictorial and verbal beauty that it almost makes us
forget the romantic thinness of the human emotions.
Here 'sensations' remain largely aesthetic and material sensations. *La Belle Dame sans Merci*, whether
or not we give it a personal significance, may be
called both an anti-romantic reply to *The Eve of
St. Agnes* and a piece of romantic magic. The baleful
love of a fairy for a mortal had been a theme of old
ballads (though Keats seems to have in mind the
first book of *The Faerie Queene*), but this blend of
love and beauty and evil is nearer to *Christabel*. With
these poems and the unfinished *Eve of St. Mark*,
which is distinctive in its precise, restrained detail,
Keats paid his tribute to medievalism.

But most of Keats's good poetry, and some that
is not so good, is more serious and complex than the
romantic narratives. We have observed the self-
consciousness that led Wordsworth to plan and partly
write a vast poem on his own development, and
parallel motives worked on Keats, in less openly
personal ways. From the sonnet on Chapman's
Homer to *The Fall of Hyperion*, almost all of his
major and many minor poems deal with the nature

and problems of the poet. That in itself is a remarkable fact.

There is the further fact that Greek myth and, to a smaller extent, Greek art and literature provide either his main themes or numerous allusions. Keats's boyish enthusiasm had been nourished by his Elizabethan reading, by Leigh Hunt, by the Elgin Marbles, and, again, by Wordsworth. One reason for Keats's high regard for *The Excursion* would be the account in the fourth book of the Greek religion of nature and its imaginative expression in myth. Classical myth, which had been so rich an element in Renaissance poetry from Spenser to Milton, had been blighted by Augustan rationalism, but it revived with the romantic religion of nature and the imagination. Blake, who hated the classics and invented, with occult aids, his own mythology, was the only major poet who did not turn to classical myth, and even he made some disguised use of it. If it were not for the bond between myth and nature, we might think such symbols quite alien to Wordsworth, but, in addition to the passages in *The Excursion*, there is such an impassioned sonnet as 'The world is too much with us', which Keats had echoed in *Sleep and Poetry*: the Greeks, who saw Proteus rising from the sea and heard old Triton blow his wreathed horn, were nearer religion than Christian Englishmen intent on money, with no eye or ear for nature. (As a small reminder of the renewed vitality of the older poets, we may note that Wordsworth's Proteus and Triton came from Spenser.)

In poems both early and late Keats is a true romantic in seeking, through nature and myth, the senses and imagination, to 'burst our mortal bars', to win a vision of reality. In *Endymion* he uses the 'Platonic' fable of Drayton's poem, whether he knew that work or not. The hero, leaving action for contemplation, pursues the ideal, learns the lessons of harmony with nature, humanitarian service, and love, and eventually finds that the way to the ideal is through the real, that the two are identical. Yet the axiom had not been proved on the author's pulses, and the problem was resumed in *Hyperion*. Spenser had used the war of the gods and Titans to pose the question of providential, ordered evolution or naturalistic disorder; Keats sees the naturalistic progress of the race and the poet. Apollo becomes a god when he has comprehended the pains of existence. The great and less great odes of the spring of 1819 are variations on the same essential theme. Outwardly, in the *Nightingale* and the *Grecian Urn*, the immortality of art is set above the fleeting actualities of experience, yet the poet feels both the joys and the sorrows of life too keenly to find escape and assurance in the ideal; even while he glorifies the One, his instincts cleave to the Many. In the second version of *Hyperion* Keats is tortured by his own questionings of the nature and value of poetry; but what he sees in the unveiled face of Moneta is an answer that seems to rise from pagan towards Christian myth, that seems to reconcile art and action, joy and sorrow, the ideal and the actual, immortality and mortality. Whether or not Keats had attained this kind of serenity, in his last great utterance, *To Autumn*, he has put aside all tormenting problems and is enjoying the serenity of purely sensuous contemplation.

Thus Keats's themes raise, almost always in symbolic and poetic terms, questions that his fellow poets seldom asked; and while these questions have their romantic roots and colouring, they transcend their age and reappear in Victorian and modern poets. But Keats was not only a deeply thoughtful poet, he was also the most studious and inspired artist among the romantics. He took a long time—as time is reckoned in the Keatsian calendar—to work free of both his own erratic taste and bad influences, and even his mature poems were not always flawless. The massive sonnet on Chapman's *Homer*, the spontaneous product of an exciting experience, stands out from a great deal of poor apprentice work. And in the longer poems up through *Isabella*, momentary felicities stand out from thin, wayward, and often meretricious lushness and general lack of style and form. *Hyperion* (1818–19) was the first long poem in which, with no fumbling or bathos, Keats displayed sure taste and sustained control— and not only that but a majesty of style and movement that even the hostile Byron pronounced as sublime as Aeschylus. It is something of a paradox that Keats's first great work of art should have been a *tour de force* in a manner that, despite imitation, is not Miltonic and yet is not his own. But in the fragment of objective epic he had not, unless at the end, got said what he wanted to say, and when he came to recast the poem he turned to Dante (in Cary's translation) as a model for a personal-symbolic induction; and now he achieved a style that was at once new and his own. In the rewritten part of the first version, we may think he lost far more than he gained, yet he was evidently willing to sacrifice much for more rigorously functional expressiveness.

The first mature poem in his natural manner was *The Eve of St. Agnes*. Keats's minute revisions in this and the first *Hyperion*, and in other works, provide, as all students know, an education in poetry. They show him, as W. J. Bate in particular has demonstrated, replacing relatively flat or feeble words with suggestive and forcible ones, especially in the way of epithets and verbs, in general obtaining heightened intensity, and accomplishing parallel effects in rhythm. The *Ode to a Nightingale*, as the anecdote tells us, was an astonishing *ex tempore* production, though the complex stanzas of this and the other odes apparently grew out of Keats's prolonged experiments with the sonnet and his recent use of the Spenserian stanza in *The Eve of St. Agnes*. When he returned in *Lamia* (1819) to the long narrative, he wrote, not with the straggling looseness and prodigality of *Endymion*, but in the strong, compact, forward-moving couplets of Dryden's *Fables*; here Keats's technical and verbal brilliance seems to cover an uncertain attitude towards his theme. In his valediction, *To Autumn* (1819), the least ambitious and most perfect of the great odes, poetry comes as naturally as the leaves to a tree, and surprises by a fine excess.

While the quality of Keats's best poems and his whole approach to poetry have kept him relatively immune from the anti-romantic reaction of our day, Shelley (1792–1822) has been the whipping-boy of modern criticism. An age that has insisted on precision and particularity cannot abide Shelley's notorious vagueness and abstraction. Besides,

although some modern poets and critics have had
an active social conscience, Shelley's crusading
humanitarianism and his general outlook on poetry
and life have not been congenial. It might have been
expected that devotees of Blake would be devotees
of Shelley, and vice versa, since both are foes of
priests and kings and repressive authority and
proclaim a roughly similar gospel of love and liberty,
and since Blake's prophetic material and manner are
certainly not less vague, for the inexpert reader, than
Shelley's; yet the two poets appear in the main to
have distinct tribes of followers.

It is no less obvious, and more logical, that few
persons are drawn equally to Shelley and Keats.
To one party—and the writer of this book must in
candour avow that he belongs to it—Shelley, with
all his manifest intellectual and poetic power, seems
for the most part to be a peculiar and unsatisfying
blend of the prophetic and realistic with the immature and nebulous. As many critics have said in
one way or another, Keats's experience and wisdom
fit into our own, while Shelley, despite his concern
for humanity, is a remote, unearthly visitant from a
heaven both 'Platonic' and private. Do we read
Shelley's chief poems in the same spirit in which we
read Keats's, as timeless, inexhaustible poetry, or do
we read them, even *Prometheus Unbound*, rather as
documents of English romanticism or Shelleyan
Platonism or Shelleyan biography?

Parallels and contrasts between Keats and Shelley
run all through their temperaments and their writing.
Shelley's education and environment saved him from
some of Keats's early disadvantages (though not from
a streak of sentimentality or the charnel-house

images of Gothic romanticism). The philosophy
of Godwin, if in some sense an inspiration, was
a heavier liability than the aesthetic influence of
Hunt was for Keats. Shakespeare, the creator of men
and women, who meant everything to Keats, meant
very little to Shelley; even *The Cenci* is a drama of
Evil versus Good. To Keats, Milton was chiefly
the great artist; Shelley, though he echoed Milton's
language, saw him as the great rebel. Both Keats
and Shelley cherished their own versions of Wordsworth's religion of nature, but for Keats Wordsworth was above all the poet of the human heart,
while for the young Shelley the poet of nature and
truth and liberty was a lost leader. The Keats who
resented the doctrinaire Wordsworth could not find
Shelley less so, and in his late letter to Shelley
advised him to curb his magnanimity and be more
of an artist.

Shelley's first long poem, *Queen Mab* (1812–13),
embodied his revolutionary and metaphysical doctrines; Keats's first long poems were about poetry.
Shelley's next important work, *Alastor* (1815), was a
very romantic parable of the frustration and death
of the idealist poet in quest of human love and
sympathy, a parable to which *Endymion* may have
been, or may be read as, an answer. Shelley could
not, like Keats, identify the ideal with earthly
reality. The two poems are no less characteristic in
texture than in theme. *Endymion*, though visionary,
and diffuse, is concrete in its multitudinous details;
in *Alastor* concrete details are lost in the phantas-
magoria of the whole. In general, though Keats has
'a mighty abstract Idea of Beauty', the abstraction
is less real to him than particular beautiful things.

For Shelley the abstraction is more real than any particulars (unless perhaps these are women, and even they are partly abstract). Keats could hardly have written a *Hymn to Intellectual Beauty*. Keats's nightingale is there in the garden, and his lines move slowly under a weight of both substantial sensations and serious questioning of life and death and art; Shelley's skylark, a bird of the air, is lost in a shower of iridescent, half-abstract images, and, while the feeling of joyous song is rendered with spontaneous exuberance, allusions to human suffering seem almost inconsequential. The *Ode to the West Wind* (1819) is no less different from Keats's odes. Shelley's interwoven images of wind and swift motion are as typical as Keats's palpable images of stillness. And while Keats, meditating on the relations of art and human life, presents conflicts of uncertain outcome, Shelley is illustrating an idea, humanitarian revolution, that he is already committed to. Shelley has nothing of the negative capability that Keats coveted and in some degree attained. Shelley does not see an object or emotion in itself but partly as an idea, and behind all ideas is a vision of infinity and harmonious oneness that starts far beyond the actualities of experience. Thus Shelley commonly demands much more sympathy with his 'meaning' than Keats, whose direct sensuous apprehension and power of communication could, one imagines, capture a reader who had the misfortune to be indifferent to his ideas.

This special demand on the reader lessens at times, notably when Shelley's remarkable myth-making instinct has relatively free play. He can become the cloud, or Apollo, or Alpheus and

Arethusa, or Pan (though Pan is a frustrated lover more Shelleyan than shaggy); and one might add that complex but playful and graceful poem on the poetic imagination, *The Witch of Atlas* (1820), written in the vein of Shelley's translations of the Homeric Hymns. But in many lyrics, and in some of his longer poems that are lyrical in spirit, the author's vision, amatory, humanitarian, or metaphysical, lapses into the revery of idyllic wish-fulfilment or self-pity. There are exceptions of course. To mention only two, 'Life of Life! thy lips enkindle' carries abstractions to a rare pitch of intensity; and in Shelley's 'Messianic eclogue', 'The world's great age begins anew' (which in turn inspired one of Yeats's finest lyrics), radiant hopes end in a moving cry of despair. But such lyrics on poetry and love as 'On a poet's lips I slept' and 'My soul is an enchanted boat' (both in *Prometheus Unbound*), especially when put beside parallel passages in Plato's *Symposium* and *Ion*, and *Statesman* respectively, suggest the melting of serious myths into day-dreams. We, having grown up on seventeenth-century poetry, like bone and muscle, and Shelley has little of either. We often wish for something of the plain vigour that found vent chiefly in Shelley's journalistic verse—'An old, mad, blind, despised, and dying king.'

Prometheus Unbound (1818–19) and Keats's unfinished *Hyperion* are the pre-eminent examples of the romantics' revival of Greek myth. Prometheus was a favourite theme of continental romanticism, and Byron had already put into the Titan's mouth one of his defiances of heaven. Shelley's lyrical drama is a vision, akin to Blake's, of humanity's emancipation from the tyranny of Jupiter, who represents the religious, moral, and political shackles that man has forged for himself. Progress is a subsidiary theme in *Hyperion*, and it is treated in generalized and aesthetic terms. If Jupiter and Prometheus are Shelley's usual black and white, one of Keats's difficulties is that his gods could hardly surpass the nobility of his chief Titans. But both poets, in their opposed groups and figures, are objectifying the process and conflicts of individual growth. Keats's central theme is Apollo's becoming a god, a mature poet, through his realization of the ills of the world; and Jupiter's real overthrow occurs when love supersedes hate in the regenerated soul of the suffering Prometheus. Thus there is some affinity, but still more dissimilarity.

While Shelley had a knowledge of Greek that Keats had not, he naturally did not choose to follow Aeschylus very far in theme or structure. Aeschylus's solution, that ultimately Prometheus and Zeus would each learn moderation and wisdom and be reconciled, was of course abhorrent to the Manichean revolutionary. And the normal texture of his poetry is hardly less un-Greek. What elements of concreteness there are appear chiefly in the first act. For the most part Shelley's personages are indistinct phantoms and mouthpieces compared with those of either *Prometheus Bound* or *Hyperion*, where the setting is substantial and the characters are simply superhuman. Asia is one of Shelley's many symbols of Nature, Love, and Beauty, and her reunion with Prometheus is the restoration of harmony between nature and man and within man. Although Shelley had been moving from Godwinism toward a kind of Platonism, the millennium he envisions is still Godwinian: the abolition of priests, kings, marriage, and other restraints leaves man exempt from awe, guilt, and pain, and free to exercise his natural virtue. But Shelley's vision is not limited to the moral regeneration of man and society; it is also Baconian. Perfected man will learn to control the forces of nature. Shelley's faith in science, like his amateurish but considerable knowledge, goes far beyond that of the other romantic poets (Keats's medical training hardly touched his poetry); indeed many images in the drama that look at first like bubbles of Shelleyan gas have been shown to be scientific. Finally, although he longed for a perfect world, Shelley could not of course admit the Christian Deity as a symbol or guarantee of an ultimate triumph of right. Instead he sets up the shadowy Demogorgon, who dethrones Jupiter and who is given the concluding speech, of which the last stanza provides the standard conclusion for essays on Shelley. It, and the drama as a whole, have often been said to embody the teaching of Christ, a view that may puzzle many readers.

The impassioned urgency of *Adonais* (1821) springs from the elegist's weeping his own fate in another's, but what resemblance the poem has to *Lycidas* ends there. The lack of concrete substance and edge; the diffuse, rhetorical, and artificial handling of the myth of Adonis and the Greek pastoral conventions; the quite factitious use of the author's friends, Byron and Moore, as mourners; the shrillness of the attack on the reviewers; the sentimentalizing of Keats and the egotistic sentimentalizing of Shelley himself (he and his heroes must always be pallid weaklings in a brutal world)—all this makes a sad contrast with the control, the 'decorum', the impersonality, the central conflict, and the substantial beauty of *Lycidas*. *Adonais* is no doubt partly redeemed by the conclusion, where, soaring beyond the world of wrong and death, Shelley celebrates the poet's immortal oneness with the nature he made more lovely.

In his last work, the unfinished *Triumph of Life* (1822), a partial parallel to *The Fall of Hyperion*, Shelley's despair is relieved only by the thought of Plato and Bacon and 'the sacred few'—presumably such pure spirits as Socrates and Jesus—who 'touched the world with living flame'. The poem as a whole is a pageant of the corrupt many, conquerors and conquered, deceivers and deceived, the multitude who have served the Mammon of unrighteousness. We might not expect Voltaire and Rousseau in such a throng, a Rousseau, moreover, who is conscious of having benefited mankind and of having been overcome, not, like the rest, by Life, but by his own extravagant heart. The poem is a moving arraignment of human history, a moving reassertion of the poet's ideals, and yet, in being such, it proves more clearly than any other work of his that he could not escape from insubstantial fluency, since here if anywhere we might look for bone and muscle. Like Keats in his last testament, Shelley has Dante in mind (as well as Petrarch's *Trionfi*), but even in this poem the lines that well up from profoundly disenchanted bitterness of spirit have much of his usual light and thin transparency. He cannot help singing (though his voice is subdued), when he needs weighted speech.

In the early decades of the nineteenth century Byron (1788–1824) was first and the other romantic poets nowhere; and he was the only one who made an impact on the Continent, both in his own day and for a long time afterwards. Of the cloud of witnesses, none defined Byron's earth-shaking power more succinctly than Arnold, in his *Memorial Verses* (1850) on Wordsworth and *Stanzas from the Grande Chartreuse* (1855):

> *When Byron's eyes were shut in death,*
> *We bow'd our head and held our breath.*
> *He taught us little: but our soul*
> *Had felt him like the thunder's roll.*
> *With shivering heart the strife we saw*
> *Of Passion with Eternal Law;*
> *And yet with reverential awe*
> *We watch'd the fount of fiery life*
> *Which serv'd for that Titanic strife.*
>
> *What helps it now, that Byron bore,*
> *With haughty scorn which mock'd the smart,*
> *Through Europe to the Aetolian shore*
> *The pageant of his bleeding heart?*
> *That thousands counted every groan,*
> *And Europe made his woe her own?*

Although in the second passage Byron is dismissed as of no avail to modern man (we recall Carlyle's earlier 'Close thy *Byron*; open thy *Goethe*'), in his essay of 1881 Arnold put Wordsworth and Byron at the head of the romantic poets. Keats, he said, had probably a more consummate poetic gift than either, but he died too young; Coleridge was 'wrecked in a mist of opium'; Shelley was a 'beautiful and ineffectual angel, beating in the void his luminous wings in vain'. But 'Wordsworth and Byron stand out by themselves. When the year 1900 is turned, and our nation comes to recount her poetic glories in the century which has then just ended, the first names with her will be these.'

This prophecy was not fulfilled in 1900 and holds still less perhaps for 1952. Byron is on the whole an extinct volcano. The force of his personality and the glamour of his career remain a fascinating phenomenon that calls forth innumerable biographies, and he takes a pre-eminent place in any picture of the early nineteenth century, yet of his writing little outside the satires and the letters still has a life of its own. We are all aware of 'the Byronic hero' (who was older than Byron or Mrs. Radcliffe), but nobody would embark on the romantic narratives that Byron scribbled in the intervals of his London dissipations; one exception might be the late, short, and different *Mazeppa*. Nobody reads the dramas, in which Byron was partly following Alfieri. We have in our minds some lyrics, such as *She Walks in Beauty* and *So, We'll Go No More A-Roving* (not to mention 'The Assyrian came down like a wolf on the fold'); and *Prometheus*, the shortest and most impressive statement of Byron's quarrel with the Calvinistic Jehovah; and if we have no clear memory of *The Prisoner of Chillon*, at least we have seen the castle. When we are 'doing the romantic movement', we look through some minor things and read, with a modicum of inward commotion, the third and fourth cantos of *Childe Harold's Pilgrimage* (1816–18) and *Manfred* and *Cain*. In *Manfred* (1817) the Byronic hero has become a darker embodiment of nameless guilt (nowadays no longer nameless, though the poet's experience was blended with Gothic convention). *Cain* (1821) may be called a large-scale *Prometheus*. Though he rebelled against it, Byron had a sense of sin that was deficient in some of the other romantic poets.

As Byron's wit (another quality lacking in his fellow poets) and his championship of Pope remind us, he was in part a man of the rational and rhetorical eighteenth century. *Childe Harold*, for all its personal world-weariness, was in the tradition of the old descriptive and reflective poem. With Napoleon under lock and key, travellers were bowling about Europe, and Byron supplied a highly readable Baedeker, describing the Waterloo Ball and delivering eloquent speeches to mountains and the sea, the Coliseum and three-starred statues. If his sensibility and expression are unmistakably of the romantic age, he can make us think of such things as, say, Thomson's *Liberty*. Like the earlier poets, he gets his effects—much stronger effects than theirs— by the page rather than by the line or the phrase. In other words, he has a fatal want of concentration and distinction of style. We can still feel something of the force and fire that enabled him, without becoming absurd, to apostrophize the grand monuments of nature and art, but he was only rarely and by accident a poet. His qualities, good and bad, are those of a rhetorician. That is one reason why he may lose little, and even gain, in being translated, whereas a translation of Keats is impossible—though foreign critics attempt it.

Byron was the last of the gentlemen who wrote with ease, and satire was a genre that brought out his best gifts and made his slipshod facility less conspicuous. *The Vision of Judgment* (1822) is a masterpiece of agile wit and tone. So too is *Don Juan* (1819–24), though it has its dull passages. As a successor, in the romantic age, to the old heroic poem, a comic epic was much less logical than *The Prelude*, but, if such a thing was to be written, it could be done only by the ex-lion of London society, the hero of many scandals, the cosmopolitan aristocrat who had been everywhere and seen and done everything, and who could look back with amused or angry contempt at the levity, vacuity, and hypocrisy of the life he had shared. The social, literary, and political sophistication and wit of the brilliant letter-writer are channelled into stanzas and a style of colloquial energy. Whatever he learned from Pulci and Hookham Frere, Byron made the medium his own. Some of the best-known parts, of course, are not satirical—the grim shipwreck, the idyll of Haidée and Juan—though Byron can flick these episodes with mockery. And the impassioned rhetoric of 'The Isles of Greece' carries us to Missolonghi. Yet Byron's final, noble gesture cannot elevate his love of freedom into either philosophic wisdom or philosophic anarchism; his impatience of all restraint extended to nations the liberty he wanted for himself.

Instead of the general summary with which this chapter should end, we must take the briefest glance at a figure whose turbulence, unlike Byron's, shook only those in his immediate vicinity, and whose literary presence we are apt to forget, that is, Walter Savage Landor (1775–1864). Landor's writings in verse and prose, English and Latin, covered nearly seventy years. He published *Gebir*, an epic of rather cryptic density, in the year of *Lyrical Ballads*, and lived to receive, as an aged libertarian and neo-pagan, the excited homage of Swinburne. As a person and an author, Landor belonged to the eighteenth century, the romantic age, and the Victorian age, and in all three periods he was a lion who walked by himself. He was an eighteenth-century aristocrat and a republican; a romantic poet whose theory and practice were classical; a man of explosive personality and opinions whose poetry was austerely impersonal and almost sufficiently detached from life and ideas to be called 'pure poetry' or Imagism.

But these and other paradoxes are resolved in the central fact that Landor's highest and most compelling ideal was literary and technical. While the romantic and early Victorian poets wrote with Elizabethan prodigality and colour, Landor, setting before himself such models as Pindar, strove for the compact and 'diaphanous'—not, however, because he believed, with the young Arnold, that the high and heavy spiritual responsibility of poetry required bare strength, but because he felt no such responsibility and cherished a pseudo-classical notion of form and style as ends in themselves. Many of Landor's poems treat classical myths, but whereas for the other poets myths are symbols charged with meaning, Landor is usually content to retell the stories, and usually without much human interest. The craftsmanship that shuns the realities of experience, and concentrates on expression when there is little to express, is not even facing the problems of the craftsman. Thus, though critics periodically deplore the neglect of Landor, we cannot really say, in spite of a few fine poems, that neglect is unjustified.

Finally, perhaps the best summary of romantic achievements and shortcomings will be an attempt to see what the Victorian poets were able and eager to carry on, and what they modified or rejected or lost.

CHAPTER V

THE VICTORIAN AGE

THE Victorian age covered a wider span than even the good queen's long reign. It may be said to have extended from about 1829–33, the time of the first real development of railways, the Catholic Emancipation Act, the first Reform Bill, the abolition of slavery, the beginning of the Oxford Movement, and the publication of Lyell's *Principles of Geology*, to the eve of the First World War. Not of course that those eighty-odd years were all of a piece; but, in comparison with the periods before and since, they had a relatively stable continuity and character. Yet, if we, who have had two world wars and have come to accept international conflict and chaos as normal, look back on the Victorians as placid and comfortable, we make a serious error. International enmities and scientific slaughter (with which they had some acquaintance) are not the only spectres that can dismay mankind, and the many great and less great Victorians furnish abundant evidence of outward and inward disturbance and suffering.

The Victorian poetical scene is as crowded as Frith's painting of Derby Day, and a multitude of minor poets must be neglected. Moreover, the chief works and general character of the major poets are relatively familiar to everyone, and what little can be said here may be focused on four topics: the Victorians' partial acceptance and modification of their romantic inheritance; their reactions to the social, religious, and philosophical problems of a progressive, sceptical, and scientific age; their conception of the place and function of the poet in the modern world; and the aims and qualities of their poetic art. These related topics, to be sure, embrace almost everything, but the discussion of them will not.

Among the few authentic poets who arose in the early Victorian age one cause of depression might well have been the low estate of poetry and of public taste. In literate circles, in and outside the universities, the great romantics had come into their own (and Byron had always been a force), but an unsophisticated public fed on a thin and decorous romanticism and edifying pietism. When Tennyson and Browning were publishing their early volumes, there were a number of respectable or distinctive minor poets, survivals or new arrivals, such as Leigh Hunt, John Clare, George Darley, Hartley Coleridge, Thomas Hood, Elizabeth Barrett, Thomas Lovell Beddoes (though *Death's Jest Book* did not appear till 1850); but the standard poets on the drawing-room table were likely to be Campbell and Moore, Mrs. Hemans and 'L. E. L.', Keble and Sir Henry Taylor. And versifiers now forgotten were even more popular. Macaulay wielded his vorpal sword in vain upon the religious poems of Robert Montgomery; Robert Pollok's *The Course of Time* (1827), an epic culminating with the terrors of the Judgment, reached its seventy-eighth thousand in 1868; and from 1838 onward Martin Tupper was putting forth slices of his *Proverbial Philosophy*. If we avert our eyes from *The May Queen, Enoch Arden*, and the like, we should remember how often and how greatly Tennyson rose above popular taste, and how much he did to raise it. Moreover, until the advent of Arnold, the authoritative criticism of the great reviews was both forcible and feeble; such policemen of letters as Croker and John Wilson, who had bludgeoned Keats, were there to give a similar welcome to Tennyson.

The two supreme problems that confronted the serious Victorian mind were both born of science, the industrial revolution and the religious revolution. The industrial revolution, while making England the workshop of the world, was yielding a full and growing harvest of wealth and misery and strife. What Carlyle called 'the condition of England' was a prime anxiety of awakened consciences among Evangelicals, Broad Churchmen, humanitarian liberals, social critics, novelists, and some poets, from Tennyson down through Mrs. Browning to Ebenezer Elliott. During the first half of the century sporadic outbreaks of violence, the Chartist movement, and other symptoms of economic distress led to real fear of revolution. But 1848, the year of European upheaval, passed, and in 1851 came the Great Exhibition, a reassuring proof of peace, prosperity, and the wonders of applied science.

Most of the romantic poets had held, with varying degrees of confidence and concreteness, a belief in progress. The Victorian poets who inherited that belief had to face a far larger body of painful and insistent facts. In general they did not offer much in the way of direct social and political comment. The important exception was Tennyson. *Locksley Hall* (1842), which does not much attract us, had, according to Charles Kingsley, 'most influence on the minds of the young men of our day' as a call to social action;

Tennyson's vision of air-borne commerce and aerial battles has been more amply fulfilled than his vision of 'the Parliament of man, the Federation of the world'. If we respond to the violently prejudiced political utterances of Byron and Shelley, we may not be stirred by Tennyson's Burkeian principles; but *Love Thou Thy Land* contains an exact picture of our present world and some deeply felt wisdom that is still wisdom. That cannot be said of the Laureate's patriotic songs. (The *Ode on the Death of the Duke of Wellington* is a mixture of editorial obituary and noble poetry.) To pass by the well-meant *Princess*, there was social comment in *In Memoriam* and angry protest in the 'spasmodic' *Maud* (1855) and *Locksley Hall Sixty Years After* (which outdid the original in bluster). The hero of *Maud*, even more than the hero of the early *Locksley Hall*, is a rebel against the Mammonism of society. In addition to its technical novelties, structural and symbolic, *Maud* is a remarkable anticipation of psychological conflicts that have become more familiar in the age of Freud and frustration. The neurotic hero is one of the mid-Victorian 'lost generation', a sort of Hemingway character (though much more conscious and complex) who oscillates between apathy and violence, love and death, self and a selfless cause.

The romantic poets, revolting against a scientific view of the world, had found reality in a religion of nature, or, more broadly, in poetic intuition. In the course of the nineteenth century the gulf between scientific rationalism and poetry only widened and deepened. While science was making immense progress, it had its own 'Fundamentalism', an obsession with mechanical law that affected even ethical

thought of the period. At any rate the Wordsworthian religion of nature could have little meaning for
most Victorians. Tennyson, a zealous student of
science from youth to old age, for the most part saw
in nature only what his acute senses or scientific
knowledge reported. One result was much accurate
and beautiful description of the varied appearances
of sky and earth and sea; another was glimpses of
nature red in tooth and claw, of a globe shifting its
contours through ages of geological change, of a
universe in which that globe was a microscopic dot.
To Browning nature was a minor interest and mainly
an occasional background for love and death and
heroic striving, but his pictures of it were characteristically sharp, rugged, and violent. Arnold at times
came nearest, if not very near, to the Wordsworthian
attitude, though he saw nature as an enemy as well
as a refuge.

But science threatened much more than the romantic religion of nature and the imagination, and the
earlier Victorian poets experienced more distress
than their predecessors because they had a stronger
family inheritance of religious belief and because the
tide of scientific scepticism had risen so much higher.
Physical science, represented by Sir Charles Lyell,
the popularizer Robert Chambers (*Vestiges of the
Natural History of Creation*, 1844), and other men up
through Darwin, Huxley, and Tyndall, developed a
picture of the world in which God seemed unneces-
sary and man irrelevant. Most of the philosophical
oracles, such as Bentham, Carlyle, Mill, and Spencer,
and multiplying exponents of the new science of
Biblical criticism, contributed in their various ways
to the undermining of Christian faith. Throughout

the Victorian age, whatever misconceptions of both religion and science were involved, there was spiritual anguish and tragedy for many of those people who were caught in the conflict—the overwhelming sense of falling from solid ground into a dark abyss, of being thrust out from filial membership in a providential order into a meaningless universe of natural law or chaos, of having to turn from belief in immortality to the idea of the final dissolution of lumps of carbon and water. Although many people could embrace the secular 'religion of humanity', and some Anglo-Catholicism, others, with the ebbing of the sea of faith, remained in shivering loneliness on the naked shingles of the world.

But we must leave background for the chief figures in the foreground, Tennyson, Browning, and Arnold.

The most representative is of course Tennyson (1809–92), whose publications ran from 1827 to the year of his death, and whose religious and metaphysical questionings covered a still longer span. In the large body of his youthful verse (some of the most precocious was not printed until 1930–31), there was a marked vein of more than normal adolescent melancholy. Sir Charles Tennyson's biography (1949) revealed the prolonged and acute strains that home life—centring around a disinherited, embittered, and often deranged father—brought upon the sensitive boy; and, with the father's death, the young man had to leave Cambridge and steer a numerous and problematical family through difficult waters. Tennyson's sense of isolation was aggravated by concern about his poetic direction, by harsh reviews, by religious problems, and by the shock of Arthur Hallam's death.

For one thing, the legacy he inherited from the romantic poets was an already embarrassed one. Even while they had been declaring their faith in the poetic imagination, in the almost divine office of the poet, the doctrine had gained ground that poetry was essentially primitive and must inevitably decay with the progress of science and civilization; and civilization was becoming more and more dominated by Gradgrinds and Bounderbys. In Tennyson's Cambridge prize poem, *Timbuctoo* (1829), the spirit of imagination, the creator of the body of fable by which man has lived, anticipates the shrinking of her fair palace, under the pressure of 'keen Discovery', into mud-walled huts, barbarian settlements. A remarkable number of his early poems, among them some of his best, deal with personal or poetic isolation or both, and with the dilemma of aesthetic detachment and social responsibility. There are *Mariana*; *The Poet*, which expresses a messianic and, one might say, Shelleyan confidence (though *The Defence of Poetry* was not yet published); *The Poet's Mind*; that extraordinary incantation, *The Hesperides*, which seems to celebrate precious seclusion; *The Lady of Shalott*, in part a parable of the cloistered artist encountering actuality; *Œnone*; *Tithonus*, perhaps the most splendid and moving of Tennyson's classical poems; and those pieces in which conflicting claims are openly debated, *The Lotos Eaters*, *The Palace of Art*, and *Ulysses*. If sometimes the elaborate beauty of style might suggest lack of complete seriousness, the reality of the poet's inward tensions is shown by the persuasive power with which he could present the case for aesthetic retreat from the world. In short, Tennyson went through, in his own way, the conflict of poetic aims that had tormented Keats.

Tennyson's youthful consciousness of the religious problem was of course greatly intensified by the death of Hallam (1833). Although Hallam was a dearly beloved friend, as Edward King had not been for Milton, the extinction of a promising life crystallized for the later as for the older poet the whole question of God's government of the world and the destiny of man; but two centuries of scientific rationalism had made an affirmative answer much more difficult. Tennyson's first reactions could vary from the suicidal mood of *The Two Voices* to the resolution of *Ulysses*, from vain longing for the dead man in *Break, Break, Break* to vain longing for his own death in *Tithonus*; and *In Memoriam* (1850) contained the lyrical meditations of seventeen years.

Victorian readers welcomed *In Memoriam* as a much-desired reconciliation of science and religion, but our generation responds more fully to Tennyson's utterances of stark despair. Astronomy, geology, and biology join to picture a boundless, timeless world of natural law or anarchy that has no place for God or man, no concern with man's physical survival or his traditional beliefs and aspirations. Tennyson's answers, his attempts to find some faith to live by, are of quite different kinds. He did look, through a long future, for the evolutionary progress of man to higher levels of being (he was not dealing with the problem of the origin of species that had occupied biologists and was to be expounded by Darwin in 1859). If nowadays we look askance at ideas of progress, some such faith had animated the march of mind ever since Bacon; and, though Tennyson's 'larger hope' had a partly religious basis, it was no more vague than Hardy's melioristic hope (nor was Tennyson's vision of a Godless world less bleak and grim). But Tennyson's most earnest affirmation rested on the evidence of his own consciousness; the human capacity for love is an unshakable reality that attests a greater reality beyond the human grasp. Whatever modern positivists may say, that may be thought a tenable position. Tennyson was not, apparently, a quite orthodox Christian; in 'the night of fear' he clung with passionate intensity to two supreme convictions, a providential Deity and individual immortality.

Idylls of the King (including the early *Morte d'Arthur*), which bulked so large in Tennyson's later work, and which especially made him a popular prophet, are not much read in our time. The handling of the romantic material and the spiritual allegory—'Sense at war with Soul'—and the stylized elegance are alike unreal to us. King Arthur seems to wear the white flower of a blameless life in the lapel of a Prince Albert. Yet, in the midst of artifice, Tennyson can still paint nature, and his pictures of a society in decay have their moments. *The Holy Grail* is impressive as a whole, as a Victorian *Waste Land*, in its presentation of decadence and neurosis, the quest of spurious spirituality and excitement.

We are inclined to have a mental image of the older Tennyson, the uniquely famous oracle of the English-speaking world, but it is well to remember that *In Memoriam* and many of the best short poems were written by a poor, lonely, obscure, and profoundly troubled young man. We should remember, too, that in his later years he produced many fine things, both typical and novel, and that, for all the outward security and adulation, the poet's soul could still have glimpses of a hideous darkness. And, among the poems that testify to his rich diversity, we may recall a minor genre, his familiar addresses to friends—'Old Fitz', F. D. Maurice, Edward Lear, Mary Boyle—poems that have the easy, graceful rightness of an English Horace.

As artist, Tennyson has an imagination less dramatic than lyrical; he is usually at his best when he is kindled by personal emotion, personal experience. But this, like other generalizations we are tempted to make, is open to many exceptions. It is at any rate indisputable that he was not only a master of style and rhythm but a master of various styles and rhythms; these range from, say, the delicately evocative and elusive *Hesperides* to the solid earthiness of the *Northern Farmer*. In two areas in particular Tennyson achieved almost unfailing felicity, the poems on classical subjects and the large body of lyrics; and he worked in both veins from youth to old age. In charging classical themes with his own feelings and ideas Tennyson was especially in the Keatsian tradition. He was Keatsian also in the deliberate richness, not unmixed with deliberate simplicity, that characterizes these poems, and in the blank verse of most of them; the slow movement, in which the line is the dominant unit, is more Keatsian than Miltonic. The inlaid beauty of Tennyson's phrasing, the impression it gives of conscious composition, is even more Virgilian than Keatsian. Virgilian too is 'the passion of the past', the *lacrimae rerum*, that weighted *Tears, Idle Tears* and many other notable lyrics. Love, the universal theme of lyric poetry, inspired the ecstasies and the grief of the lover of Maud, but most of Tennyson's lyrical verse gives utterance, to quote Newman's saying about Virgil, 'as the voice of Nature herself, to that pain and weariness, yet hope of better things, which is the experience of her children in every time'. Since he was more of a lyrist than a metaphysician, it was well that *In Memoriam* grew as a sequence of lyrics. Even in that work, with its relative uniformity of ritualistic tone, Tennyson moves between the ornate and the simple. His simplicity, to be sure, may, like his ornateness, be contrived, but in most contexts contrivance of each kind may be appropriate and effective. *In Memoriam* contains, too, a good deal of studied periphrasis and studied condensation; both habits of mind can resemble 'metaphysical wit' and, as in the metaphysicals themselves, can be hazardous.

Robert Browning (1812–89) was apparently less plagued than Tennyson by questions about the nature of poetry and the function of the poet, but he did feel them; and his formulations and answers, like Tennyson's, carry on from the romantics. Two prose documents are the essays on Chatterton (*Foreign Quarterly Review*, July, 1842) and Shelley (1852); as Donald Smalley, the editor of the former, has said, Browning in both essays was intent upon viewing a romantic rebel as a prodigal son of evangelism. In the very introspective *Pauline* (1833), Browning himself was a sort of reclaimed prodigal, exposing his youthful struggle against scepticism and egocentricity. In the more objective and assured *Paracelsus* (1835) he set forth some main tenets of what was to be his lifelong creed. Paracelsus the scientist—

Browning already has an instinct for the out-of-the-way and dubious hero—has pursued knowledge without love, and Aprile the Shelleyan poet has sought beauty and love without knowledge. Browning does not simply declare for poetic intuition, nor does he add two and two to make an ideal four. Both men are one-sided. But the dying scientist sees a larger truth than either had grasped: that finite man, while he aspires and evolves from below towards fuller knowledge and love, must also surrender to the infinite knowledge and love and power that stoop from above to raise him. Thus for Browning the romantic quest of the infinite—exemplified in *Alastor*—is given a Christian reinterpretation.

A related problem, which we associate with Keats rather than Shelley, is the choice between humanitarian action and aesthetic detachment. Whether or not moderns read *Sordello* (1840; revised 1863), Browning's contemporaries may be forgiven for not discerning the poet's view of the problem, since the subject of the poem had gone through various phases of growth in his mind and was wrapped in a bewildering excess of historical detail. He was to return to questions of art and the artist in *Parleyings with Certain People of Importance in their Day* (1887), but in his best work, the shorter poems of his middle years (and doubtless *The Ring and the Book* must be included among the 'best'), Browning concentrated on dramatic and psychological studies, especially of love, religion, and art. Such practice of what was his true vocation was in keeping with the portrait of the poet in *How it Strikes a Contemporary* (1855): the curious observer of everybody's doings is one of God's spies, the town's conscience and its real master. What is here put, ironically, into the mouth of an uncomprehending gossip was to become, one might say, the hostile judgment of Yeats (a judgment anticipated by some early reviewers), that Browning saw the world as a great boarding-house with people coming and going in a confused kind of way and took their clatter and chatter as life and joy itself.

Browning dealt with problems of belief in various ways and in many poems, from *Christmas Eve and Easter Day* to *A Death in the Desert*, from *Rabbi Ben Ezra* to the Pope's speech in *The Ring and the Book*. With all his variety of material and his frequent subtlety of exposition, he may be said in general to have rung the changes on the central article of faith he had enunciated in *Paracelsus*. The dramatic ventriloquist could take account of intellectuals from Cleon to Strauss and Renan, but his answers came from his own soul, with support from his agile mind. He recoiled from a merely intellectual approach to what was a cardinal fact of his consciousness. His general position was indeed much like Tennyson's: the human capacity for love is the irrefragable proof of the all-embracing reality of divine love. Browning's faith in human and divine love carried with it his special emphasis on 'apparent failure', on the worth of aspiration, on the finite imperfection of earth and man and the infinite perfection of heaven. If Tennyson can be criticized for seeing immortality in terms of reunion with Hallam, Browning's symbols of the highest felicity are much less satisfying; he seems to envisage heaven as a scene of incessant busyness. His hearty optimism has of course long been under a cloud of damnation, and not always, perhaps, quite fairly. He did write much

besides 'God's in his heaven—All's right with the
world' (and even that is the dramatic utterance of a
simple girl); and he did not merely glorify man and
woman and love and adventurous energy but ex-
plored many twisted and damaged souls that dwelt
beyond the usual Victorian horizon. Yet the essence
of the charge remains. Much of the Browning gospel
does grate upon us. His appetite for 'solid vulgar
life' seems undiscriminating and undisciplined. For
all his studies in moral ugliness, he seems to lack a real
sense of evil. And his triumphs of religious faith seem
to be rather easily won; he has little of the despair
and naked fear that can be so moving in Tennyson.

Browning's technique, if not his sensibility, might
warrant such a label as 'the Victorian Donne', though
the parallel cannot be carried very far. Somewhat
like Donne, Browning found himself at the start
among a crowd of small poets who cultivated thin
romantic themes and a thin 'poetical' style (he was
able to admire his future wife's rather gushing vein),
and he had a strong instinct for the direct, dramatic
rendering of character and situation; and drama of
course demands realistic colloquialism of speech and
rhythm. Yet Browning's style and tone and rhythm,
while always distinctive, vary greatly with his wide
range of subject, from

> *Gr-r-r—there go, my heart's abhorrence!*
> *Water your damned flower-pots, do!*

to

> *Where the apple reddens*
> *Never pry—*
> *Lest we lose our Edens,*
> *Eve and I.*

For evidence of his rich variety one has only to recall (as with Tennyson) a random list of poems and the style and rhythm their themes evoke—the single-hearted ecstasy of Abt Vogler and the emotional tensions of *A Toccata of Galuppi's*; the artistic gifts and frustrations of the genial Fra Lippo Lippi and the defeated Andrea del Sarto; the over-ripe classical culture of Cleon and the medical lore of the humble Karshish, which are linked by the strange tale of an obscure Nazarene; and many other familiar poems. In such creations it is only now and then that the dramatic illusion is broken by the voice of the poet declaring his own creed; in some others we may be chiefly aware of Browning.

He is at his undidactic and artistic best in such a poem as *The Bishop Orders his Tomb at St. Praxed's Church*, and there is no better illustration of one source of his incomparable vividness, the concrete particulars that his minute and heterogeneous learning can assemble for the depiction of background and character. 'Peach-blossom marble', 'paltry onion-stone', 'brown Greek manuscripts', and a hundred other details bring to life the neo-pagan aestheticism of a Renaissance bishop. It can be said, roughly, that Browning's success varies with the plenitude or the paucity of such particulars. But if this power was one of his great assets, it was also, along with the power of minute psychological analysis, a liability. The reading of *Sordello* and of some later long poems is like wading through glue. On a smaller scale, there is the contrast between two such satires on aspects of Victorian religious thought as *Caliban upon Setebos* and *Bishop Blougram's Apology*: while Caliban's speculations are dramatized with animal energy and even more than Browning's usual instinct for tactile imagery, in the *Apology* particulars fail to animate what becomes a tedious tissue of dialectical subtleties and ironies. Happily a multitude of the shorter poems are triumphs of both concrete and psychological drama.

But Browning grew less and less able to select the significant and more and more the victim of his own volubility. He complained, like some other poets, of the externality of Tennyson's *Idylls*—'the castle, and the effect of the moon on its towers'—but his own late works can be no less oppressive with their rubble of both factual and psychological data. The bulldozer sweeps everything before it. Even *The Ring and the Book* would be a much better poem, and would have more and more eager readers, if it were half as long as it is. However, we may be grateful for Browning's powerful originality, which, in adding to the realm of poetry the rich territory of the novelist, added new and 'prosaic' resources to poetic language and rhythm. If the influence of his colloquial idiom was not much felt immediately, it worked upon some modern poets, notably Ezra Pound, and thereby had a share in creating the natural speech of recent poetry.

Matthew Arnold (1822–88) had much more to say than Tennyson and Browning about the general problems of the poet, and much of what he said, especially in the years of his chief poetical activity just before and after 1850, sounds like 1950. In his letters to Clough one recurring theme is the utterly arid, unpoetical character of the age, of modern civilization. What ground can a modern poet stand on? What nobility or beauty can he still see? (One may wonder, by the way, if the image in *The Future*, of the black line of cities crowding upon the river of Time, embodies a recollection of Tennyson's *Timbuctoo*, in which Arnold had early discerned poetical power.) Then, to the modern soul that seeks an integrated ethical and spiritual life, traditional religion yields no valid answers; the central convictions of Tennyson and Browning mean little to the son of Dr. Arnold. Yet in a practical world given over to bustling activity, in a metaphysical world that seems a meaningless chaos, man must achieve inward order; he must ally himself with what order he can find in the universe and in the traditional wisdom of man. Such self-discipline, however, requires the suppression of the natural, spontaneous senses and emotions of youth, although these in their very intensity seem to attest some profound kind of rightness. Above all, there is love; and while love for 'Marguerite' may entail the pangs of renunciation, love can also awaken one's buried life and bring some sense of reality and security to one lost in the dark. But Arnold had been put, and put himself, under the guidance of rigorous modern teachers and ancient Stoics, and now, past thirty, he feels three parts iced over; he could not have done otherwise, and yet—to use another of his epistolary metaphors —he has been shorn of his beams in the process. Most of Arnold's great poetry is a series of variations on this many-sided conflict, spontaneity and discipline, emotion and reason, faith and scepticism, the rich youth and the dry age of the individual and the race. A victim of modern unfaith, disintegration, complexity, and melancholy, he can only long for primitive faith, wholeness, simplicity, and happiness.

This central conflict, though Arnold did not know it, was his version of Keats's dilemma, of 'sensations' versus 'thoughts', of the artist's 'negative capability' versus the moralist's attainment of 'identity', of 'a soul'. Keats, to be sure, was a poet of sensation groping towards thought, and Arnold was a stoic hungering for a life of sensation (not that, any more than Keats, the author of *The New Sirens* craved mere excitement). Moreover, Arnold's melancholy was greatly darkened by his very modern sense of spiritual isolation and by his religious predicament; Keats wrote no *Dover Beach* or *Stanzas from the Grande Chartreuse*. Arnold did see some of his complex tensions in Wordsworthian terms. As a lover of nature, who had grown up in the shadow of Rydal Mount, he gladly recognized the 'healing power' of Wordsworth, who in an iron time had saved the joy and wisdom of natural feeling from the desiccating intellect; and in Arnold's poetry Wordsworthian impulses are constantly active, though they bring more nostalgia than present satisfaction. At times he could turn from man's feverish busyness to the ordered movements of the stars, to the 'general Life' of nature 'Whose secret is not joy, but peace', to a half-Wordsworthian, half-Platonic vision of an ultimate source and haven of the spirit that is often symbolized by 'the infinite sea'. But in sterner moods he could declare that Wordsworth had averted his ken from half of human fate, and could see nature as a cosmic force indifferent to man or as a lawless and insidious foe of man's integrity.

In various early letters and poems Arnold offers hints and judgments that add up to a view of poetry both positive and incomplete. The young 'Strayed

Reveller', intoxicated by Circe's potion, has a series of painless imaginative visions, but the poet who can express tragic experience must live through it himself. If 'Not deep the Poet sees, but wide', nevertheless Sophocles 'saw life steadily, and saw it whole'; that is, his view of life was integrated as well as comprehensive. In contrast with that, Tennyson dawdles with the painted shell of the universe, and Keats and Browning are immersed in a confused multitudinousness; such verdicts, if unfair, explain Arnold's own ideal. Yet the impossibility of that ideal is the theme of his fullest statement of the problem, *Empedocles on Etna* (1852). The philosopher is driven to suicide because he cannot achieve unity and wholeness; his sceptical intellect has dried up the springs of simple, natural feeling, and he remains an arid shell. Browning could fuse and transcend the insights of Paracelsus and Aprile (and reply to *Empedocles* in *Cleon*), but there is an unbridgeable gulf between Empedocles the elderly thinker and Callicles the young singer, who represent Arnold's conflicting impulses. The child is no longer father of the man; nor can Arnold, like Ben Ezra, grow old in the belief that 'The best is yet to be'. Incidentally, Empedocles' situation, and the contrasted figures, might have started from the early scenes of *Manfred*.

In explaining why he had withdrawn *Empedocles*, in the preface to the *Poems* of 1853, Arnold made his first public pronouncement on poetry—and inaugurated a new era in criticism. We should hardly guess, from the confident classicism of this manifesto, that he had been going through years of spiritual travail. Appealing against mere modernity of theme

and introspective self-consciousness, Arnold urges
the timeless supremacy of great actions, noble characters, and intense situations. Further, whereas
Keats and others have revived Elizabethan richness,
modern poetry, with its increasing weight of spiritual
responsibility, must (as Arnold had written to
Clough) be very plain, direct, and severe. However
sound his magisterial arguments, Arnold himself
lives as a poet of introspection, not in the works
written to exemplify a theory. *Balder Dead* is simply
tedious; *Sohrab and Rustum*, fine as it is in composition and details and in the grandly symbolic (and
un-Homeric) conclusion, is the story of a distressing
accident rather than the classical tragedy it was
intended to be; and the drama *Merope* quite misses
tragic significance. Yet Arnold's critical creed, early
and late, was a consistent whole. Poetry is an art,
which must give aesthetic pleasure. But it is also
a criticism of life; the much-discussed phrase presumably meant pretty much what Arnold had said
of Sophocles. And when he looked in poets for 'high
seriousness', he was not (*pace* Mr. Trilling) looking for
'solemnity'; he was looking for the finest art combined with the fullest and deepest insight, such as he
found in Homer and Dante and Shakespeare.

We must turn back to the poems. When we consider Tennyson, Browning, and Arnold as artists,
we may alter the title of Bagehot's essay to 'Ornate,
Grotesque, and Plain in English Poetry', though
all three labels must be largely qualified. Arnold's
characteristic and often prosaic plainness came in
part from his theory of poetry, in part from the
nature of his poetic gifts. In setting forth his spiritual troubles he seeks first of all to achieve a true and

adequate statement, bare of non-essential decoration (although starting with a partly symbolic scene is almost an Arnoldian formula). The reader, while moved by what is said, may feel that the writing is not inspired and inevitable, that perhaps he himself could make improvements in diction and rhythm. Though Arnold achieves beautiful and individual rhythms (not least in the free verse that he may have derived from Goethe), he has a notoriously unreliable ear; he can begin a poem, like *Memorial Verses* or the *Grande Chartreuse*, with a brisk gait and pouncing rhymes that are quite at odds with the theme and mood.

Yet Arnold might be described as a mixture of Hardy (or an ungainly Wordsworth) and Keats. His romantic instincts, his desire for 'feeling', though half-suppressed, break through the austere or prosaic surface and flower in images from nature and the simple worlds of classical and Biblical antiquity. Such a mixture is the staple Arnold. And at times he gives free rein to his elegiac-idyllic impulses, as in *The Forsaken Merman* and the later Oxford poems; in these last, the Arnoldian intellectual melancholy almost melts away into the richly Keatsian background of scenery and myth. Among the best and most characteristic examples of the lyrical and the reflective Arnold are the final song in *Empedocles* and *Dover Beach*. The former, though devoid of explicit 'ideas', is really a glowing reassertion, after the suicide of the thinker, of the rightness of simple feeling as it lived in the primitive religion of myth and nature. *Dover Beach* is a troubled and limited affirmation of the same kind; here the voice is rather that of an Empedocles who, conscious of the loss of religious faith, can still cling to love. (This poem, by the way, seems to have been written backwards, from the last paragraph, with its Thucydidean night-battle, to the extended metaphor of the sea that makes up the first part.) Of Arnold's poetry in general we might use an image that he would not have relished: a good deal of the time he writes like an aeroplane gliding, with many small bumps, along its runway, and he does not always succeed in taking off, though his intense earnestness is always impressive; but he does often rise from the ground of analysis and diagnosis into sensuous emotion and intuition, and then language, imagery, and rhythm may fuse into something that no reader could think of improving.

Austere as Arnold's own poetic ideal was, he criticized his friend Arthur Hugh Clough (1819–61) for excessive severity and didacticism. While in Arnold himself Empedocles and Callicles were both generally present, Clough might be called an Empedocles who had long forgotten youth and song (he has sometimes been taken as a distressing proof of Dr. Thomas Arnold's effect on sensitive schoolboys). We are most familiar with those short poems that, like some of Arnold's, lament a vanished faith and, in a style as bare as their theme, set up a stoic ideal of Truth and Duty. Yet Clough had his lighter side, and he showed it not merely in the 'long-vacation pastoral', *The Bothie of Tober-na-Vuolich*, but in the more elegant *Amours de Voyage*. Here, in the setting of Garibaldi's Rome, he developed, in easy conversational hexameters, a delicately ironic comedy, with much sceptical commentary on things in general, love, war, religion, 'the British female'.

In the second half of the century, while the veteran Tennyson and Browning pursued their own lines, and the social prophets, Arnold in particular, laboured to penetrate the thick skin of complacent materialism, Dante Gabriel Rossetti (1828–82) and other new poets turned their backs on a philistine world and devoted themselves mainly to art for art's sake. If their social protest was thus largely negative, we may remember the Swinburne of *Songs before Sunrise*, the Morris of *Chants for Socialists*, the Wilde of the *Ballad of Reading Gaol*, and some other writers we shall come to. But the rising poets were more inclined towards aesthetic detachment, a very literary romanticism, than towards fulfilling Arnold's demand for a criticism of life. And the poets' cult of 'pure poetry' and Beauty, which had been nourished by their own instincts and continental preceptors, found critical support in the high-priests of aestheticism, Pater and Wilde. Whereas Tennyson, Browning, and Arnold, in their different ways, had experienced the central conflicts of Keats, the Pre-Raphaelite poets responded single-heartedly to the sensuous, romantic, medieval Keats, the poet of *The Eve of St. Agnes, La Belle Dame sans Merci*, and what has often been called the first Pre-Raphaelite poem, *The Eve of St. Mark*.

If all service ranks the same with God, the classification of poets is not important, unless for the desperate author of a small book about them, and a brief survey of the latter half of the century is made next to impossible by the sheer number and diversity of figures. Even if we omit a host of minor ones, the younger generations have no Tennyson, Browning, and Arnold who stand high above the rest—though various critics might see Hopkins or Hardy or Rossetti as such giants. The new aesthetic romanticism was obviously a main line, and it might include not only the usual names from Rossetti to Yeats, but, by partial affinity, the romantic classicist Landor (who was still writing after 1850!) and FitzGerald; yet such a grouping is too loose to be helpful. Moreover, while the Oxford Movement affected the imagery and atmosphere of quite unreligious poets, it also engendered a line of devoutly religious writers, from Newman and Christina Rossetti up to the flamboyant Francis Thompson. Then, if poetry from Swinburne to Housman carried early Victorian pessimism to new depths, we must not forget the ebullient humour of Edward Lear (whom some moderns would include among poets of tragic vision), Lewis Carroll, Gilbert, and Calverley and other parodists.

The religious problems which, after 1850, still beset Tennyson and Browning, Arnold and Clough, did not exist for most of the newer poets. They were either whole-heartedly religious or, more often, whole-heartedly unreligious or irreligious. Rossetti could take over the legendary lore and picturesque concrete imagery of medieval Catholicism, but the symbols that enveloped the Blessed Damozel were only colours on his palette. Morris was devoted to everything in medieval England except its religion. Swinburne (Arnold's 'sort of pseudo-Shelley'), an heir of such diverse rebels as Landor and the Marquis de Sade, was a militant foe of the 'pale Galilean' and of all restraints. As we move up to the twentieth century, most of the poets we meet either never had any religion or lost what they had; and some found refuge in Catholicism.

The first great manifesto of Victorian neo-paganism came from Tennyson's friend, Edward FitzGerald (1809–83). His free translation, or re-creation, of Omar Khayyám (1859) stands apart from most poetry of the time; it was, indeed, unaccountably ignored until, in 1861, it was found by someone in Quaritch's penny stall and brought to the attention of Rossetti, who shared the discovery with Swinburne and others. FitzGerald's poem was no Swinburnian narcotic but a sparkling champagne. Its billowing rhythms, its seductive Oriental atmosphere, the clean-cut richness of its fresh, bright images, cast their spell whenever one opens the book. But the hedonism of Omar-FitzGerald carried with it a defiance of the Victorian Deity more arresting than Swinburne's rhetoric:

> *Oh Thou, who Man of baser Earth didst make*
> *And ev'n with Paradise devise the Snake:*
> *For all the Sin wherewith the Face of Man*
> *Is blacken'd—Man's forgiveness give—and take!*

And we may recall an image of life that is almost the same as one in the last choruses of *The Dynasts*:

> *We are no other than a moving row*
> *Of Magic Shadow-shapes that come and go*
> *Round with the Sun-illumined Lantern held*
> *In Midnight by the Master of the Show.*

Incidentally, FitzGerald's elaborate metaphor of the Potter was taken up and reinterpreted in *Rabbi Ben Ezra*—a poem that Hardy had read to him on his death-bed, along with the first of the stanzas just quoted from FitzGerald.

The *Rubáiyát*, stealing so quietly into the world, had nothing like the electric effect of *Atalanta in Calydon* (1865) and *Poems and Ballads* (1866). Swinburne (1837–1909) centred his drama in a denunciation of 'the supreme evil, God'. (Christina Rossetti pasted over the words in her copy, and Tennyson mildly asked the daemonic young man if it was fair for a Greek chorus to abuse the Deity in the style of the Hebrew prophets.) *Hertha* is cited as proof that Swinburne had, on occasion, a mature philosophic intellect, but the proof, for all its august, oracular solemnity, may be thought inadequate; if *Hertha* had been written, say, by Emerson, it might have drawn a parody from the poet who burlesqued Tennyson's *Higher Pantheism*. In general, when Swinburne rose above the raptures and languors of passion, he carried on, in his own way, the strain that had been notable in Blake and Shelley, the worship of Man as God. The gospel appears at its best in *Hertha* and the *Prelude* to *Songs before Sunrise* (1871)—'Because man's soul is man's God still . . .' On a much lower level there is the noisy nonsense of the *Hymn of Man*, 'Glory to Man in the highest! for Man is the master of things'. Whatever his and later men's sincerity, it was Swinburne who started that self-consciously heroic attitudinizing that is most familiar in Henley's 'Out of the night that covers me' and—with an intensified bitterness —in Housman.

Although John Morley described the Swinburne of *Poems and Ballads* as 'the libidinous laureate of a pack of satyrs', and Robert Buchanan assailed Rossetti as the leader of the fleshly school, the commonest modern complaint is that they were over-literary. There is, to be sure, a gulf between Swinburne's amazing fluency and Rossetti's often elaborate density, but both, if we come to them from either earlier or later poetry, may seem to have withdrawn from life, Rossetti into a gas-lit studio, Swinburne into a library of 'curiosa'. Rossetti, thanks to his 'fundamental brain-work' and creative agonies and revisions, did produce poems that exist as substantial, individual works of art; not very many of Swinburne's can be remembered except as jets of Swinburne.

Rossetti's output was not large, and it includes the translations from medieval Italian that coloured his own sensibility and style. Though all his poems bear his impress, there is variety—the celestial realism of *The Blessed Damozel*; the earthly and typically Pre-Raphaelite realism of *My Sister's Sleep*; *A Last Confession* and the rather sentimental *Jenny*, more or less in Browning's vein; such macabre balladry as *Sister Helen*; and, not to prolong the catalogue, *The House of Life*, Rossetti's central work. In these and other poems he ranges from the plain to the ornate, but the ornate is his natural medium. While he may at times remind us of Tennyson, his concentrated refinement and involution of style, especially in the sonnets, go beyond Tennyson; if we think of any English parallels, it is of Shakespeare's sonnets. The mysticism of the flesh is rendered in the grand manner, and the fleshly is in the main absorbed into intellectualized and symbolic abstractions (and occasional conceits). It must be admitted that the liturgy of love, however impassioned and even splendid, can grow languorous and suffocating, and the reader may cry out for fresh air, for Coventry Patmore's vision of marriage or the realistic analysis of Meredith's *Modern Love.*

Like Rossetti, Swinburne has a voice unmistakably his own, but, unlike Rossetti's, his poetry has no edges, and indeed almost no inside. Such images as 'the brown bright nightingale amorous' shimmer and vanish in a dazzling flood of words and rhythms; and individual words have no weight or value, the rhythm is a dithyrambic tune. It all holds a momentary intoxication, and it has been defended as aspiring, in anticipation of Pater's phrase, towards the condition of music, and as approaching the method of the Symbolists. But poetry does need more than hypnotic shimmer and sound, and it is only once in a while—as in the *Prelude*, or *Super Flumina Babylonis*, or the elegy on Baudelaire—that a generous passion gives Swinburne substance and maturity. The youthful *Atalanta* is a marvel of radiant lyricism, and of hardly less remarkable blank verse, and yet, in spite of its serious theme, it is only 'literature'. The poems that once shocked the bourgeois have subsided into a place in the history of decadent romanticism and of abnormal psychology. In general, if we read more than a page or two of Swinburne, even when he is at his best, our faculties are not so much stimulated as blurred and benumbed.

The Defence of Guenevere (1858) by William Morris (1834–96) was the first book of Pre-Raphaelite poetry, and it signalized a kind of medievalism very different from that of Tennyson's *Idylls* (1859 f.). Morris's later voluminous tales, medieval and mythological, were, unlike the *Defence*, pitched in a low key and focused at a distance; they have the dreamy charm of a verbal tapestry, but their archaic, stylized evenness of tone has something of the effect of Swinburne and water.

The unending process of convention and revolt in poetic style—which is of course only a symptom of deeper pressures—was clearly visible throughout the century. The decorative richness of Keats and Tennyson early emerged as the dominant manner. Then came such exponents of other modes as Mrs. Browning (who attained her dubious best in *Sonnets from the Portuguese*, 1850), Browning, Arnold, Clough, the 'Spasmodics' (chiefly Sydney Dobell and Alexander Smith), and FitzGerald, and such diverse, isolated, and individual writers as Beddoes, Emily Brontë, William Barnes, and R. S. Hawker. But the Keats-Tennyson convention—the label carries no disparagement of either poet in himself—remained dominant and passed into the prolonged and varied phases that are loosely termed Pre-Raphaelite. In the latter half of the Victorian age more or less 'literary' poetry was represented by *Idylls of the King* and the accumulating work of most of the newer poets, Rossetti, Morris, Swinburne, Bridges, Wilde, Lionel Johnson, Ernest Dowson, Francis Thompson, Housman, Yeats, and many others. While this tradition yielded much fine poetry (including such late pieces by Tennyson himself as the grandly typical *Demeter and Persephone* and the surprising *Voyage of Maeldune*), it was always in danger of anaemia. The imagination tended to work at several removes from life, and language developed a poetic diction of romantic and rather precious vagueness. One indication of a 'poetical' atmosphere is the treatment of nature. For the romantic poets nature had been a reality and a religion, for Tennyson and

Arnold it was a frequent inspiration; but now it was often observed through glass or in a book. For Rossetti, the painter-poet, nature—when it appeared —was likely to be pure form and colour, or a half-unreal element in the symbolism of love and death. Swinburne's rebellious and lyrical impulses responded especially to the sea, though he could paint landscape, preferably high-lighted by the breasts of nymphs and Maenads. Morris turned back from 'six counties overhung with smoke' to a bright mirage of a pastoral England. On the whole, the Muse was rather pallid and in need of blood transfusions; and from various quarters more and more conscious or unconscious rebels appeared, seeking a closer view of actuality, a stronger and less 'poetical' idiom.

Two rebels, if they can be called that, came from within the Pre-Raphaelite circle itself, Christina Rossetti (1830–94) and Coventry Patmore (1823–96). After *The Defence of Guenevere*, the next important Pre-Raphaelite book was *Goblin Market* (1862), a homely, rich, and original fantasy of innocence and evil. But Christina Rossetti stood apart from her brother and Morris and Swinburne both in her manner and in her intense religious asceticism. If her personal and poetic vision was limited, even morbid, because of her love and fear of life and love and her longing for death and heavenly peace, her inner conflicts and occasional raptures gave birth to a lyrical simplicity that is pure, direct, and poignant.

The religious and thrice-married Patmore, on the other hand, devoted himself to the celebration of marital love (*The Angel in the House*, 1854–63) and its sacramental relation to the love of God (*The Unknown Eros*, 1868–90). At first glance *The Angel in the House* may suggest only the prattle in the vicarage garden that moderns take to be one of the Victorian horrors, but Patmore was trying to render ordinary life in ordinary language, not without touches of splendour. In the later irregular odes his semi-Tennysonian manner gives way to a strongly individual fusion of plain directness with an exalted and concentrated fervour of language and image.

The Jesuit priest, Gerard Manley Hopkins (1844–89), a Roman Catholic convert like his friend Patmore, also had a harmonious vision, very much his own, of the earthly and the divine, but a vision intensified and tormented by a whole complex of inward and outward causes. His poems were first published in 1918 by Bridges, his friend and trustee (who had previously printed a few in anthologies), and since then Hopkins has been a major force in poetry and a major subject of criticism. He began, as a schoolboy, with the sharply original as well as Keatsian *Vision of the Mermaids*; his mature poetry has no or few nineteenth-century affinities, though at moments he may remind us of Patmore or Meredith. While the modern intellectual has grown more receptive to religious poetry than he used to be, thanks in part to the metaphysical revival, the interest in Hopkins has been less religious than aesthetic and technical, and recent disciples, such as Dylan Thomas, are remote from their teacher's creed.

Hopkins' bold violence in the handling of rhythm and language, which owed something to his knowledge of Greek and his acquaintance with medieval alliterative verse, went far beyond any experimentation of his century. English prosody has always allowed more or less freedom, even in ages of systematic metrics; and such different masters as Milton and Pope had, among other things, varied the number of stresses in the heroic line, while ordinarily retaining ten syllables (of which a varying proportion would be unstressed). Hopkins, going back to the still greater freedom of the alliterative patterns, combined a relatively regular number of stresses, which might be juxtaposed, with varying runs of unstressed syllables. 'Sprung rhythm' was one principal means of gaining both liberty and concentrated energy; there were others, such as a use of alliteration very different from Swinburne's. Yet, however right Hopkins' mode of utterance was for him (and he wrote to be read aloud), a reader who dwells on this side idolatry may have qualms. The lack of connective tissue and the forcible emphasis of everything can at times—as in Meredith or Carlyle— give an effect of incessant, artificial straining. Would it be blasphemy to ask if even *The Windhover*, miraculous as it is, does not distract us from its theme by some excess of violence and eccentricity?

But Hopkins does make words, familiar, unfamiliar, and freshly compounded, act as if they had never been fully alive before. His descriptive language is in the Spenserian tradition, especially the tradition of Milton and Keats, though it is as near pure Anglo-Saxon as a modern poet can get. Out of the simplest elements Hopkins can attain a very rich and individual vividness as well as strength and movement. Whatever he absorbed from his reading, poetical or theological, was completely made over into himself and became a part of his own vision. To mention one small and apparently unnoticed item, 'sheer plod makes plough down sillion Shine' is surely a religious transfiguration of Virgil's *sulco attritus splendescere vomer* (*Georg.* i. 46). At times Hopkins seems to find full release and happiness in his response to the beauty of God's creation, yet his religious joy in nature, his religious sympathy with humble men, the intensity of his devotional exaltation, did not save him from spiritual torture. Indeed his most whole-hearted devotional ecstasies reveal the quivering sensibility that found utterance in the almost hysterical despair of the 'terrible sonnets', which outdo the anguished cries of Donne.

Since Hopkins' poems were unknown outside a small circle, he had no influence. George Meredith (1828–1909), whose 'pagan' devotion to nature was comparable in fervour to Hopkins', was too strange and difficult to exert the fresh influence he might have had. During the past generation this strenuous preacher of realistic optimism has been in disrepute, while the nay-sayer Hardy has enjoyed high favour. But Meredith was and remains an original and arresting poet, as individual in style as in thought, and as intellectual in verse as in prose. He could welcome a creative view of evolution as a bracing challenge to the race. With his fusion of half-Stoic ethics and biology, his gospel of 'inspired sanity', he felt no religious loss or want; the Meredithian trinity was 'blood' (the senses and animal energies), brain, and spirit. Meredith was nature's own poet, a buoyant son of Earth. Like his sage Melampus, he was the intimate friend of all living creatures and growing things, a fearless dweller in the Woods of Westermain. Much of his best writing belongs to the outdoor world, from the early *Love in the Valley* (which some modern critics have been able to damn) to the later philosophical poems that contain his reading of earth and life. His versions of classical myth are far from the usual imitations of Tennyson; they have something of the primitive vitality of the myth-making imagination. In the more reflective poems, Meredith's ideas become clearer when we have got hold of his key-words and symbols, though his 'wit' leaps from metaphor to metaphor, or packs meta-phors together, with such speed that we may feel hustled and battered. His language can be concen-trated, sinewy, tingling with life; it can also be con-torted, muscle-bound, and ugly.

While Meredith was too highbrow to have much effect on poetic or popular taste, in the later 1880's and the 1890's the hot-house flowers of effete Pre-Raphaelitism bent before the fresh breezes of a new and robust romanticism. The crippled and explo-sive editor, W. E. Henley (1849–1903), his friend Robert Louis Stevenson (1850–94), the wandering invalid, and the bespectacled Anglo-Indian journal-ist, Rudyard Kipling (1865–1936), were men who, in fact or imagination, knew far places, who loved high romance and romantic action and England and the Empire, and who had no desire to walk down Picca-dilly with a poppy or a lily in their medieval hand. If their verse was not often significant poetry, it had a virile, timely, and wholesome tang of actuality. Henley was most original in the poems, some of them in free verse, which pictured London streets and hospital wards with colloquial and clinical realism. Kipling brought a bardic virtuosity and a gift of pictorial phrase to a multitude of 'unpoetical' sub-jects, not only Tommy Atkins and Danny Deever and M'Andrew but ships and engines and deep-sea cables. And at times he touched the hem of the true romance and of poetry.

One kind of opposition to art for art's sake came through the realistic expression of realistic pessimism (to use a crude but comprehensive word). There were such rebels against their world as James Thomson (*The City of Dreadful Night*, 1874) and John Davidson (1857-1909), who was among other things the apostle of a sort of Nietzschean Titanism. As for the very different kind of poet, A. E. Housman (1859-1936), he might take a place with the opposition by virtue of both his cynical hatred of life and his fresh, clean economy of form and style (which owed something to Shakespeare's songs and the old ballads). And yet, as his several volumes (1896, 1922, 1936) melt into one another and into the past, Housman, though he wrote some indisputably fine lyrics, seems more and more a literary poet whose stylistic and pastoral conventions have the taint of artifice. His bitterness too, however authentic in itself, carried the marks of Swinburnian neo-paganism.

The same thing may be said of a bigger poet, Thomas Hardy (1840-1928). Hardy derived his intellectual scepticism from Mill, Spencer, Darwin, and the rest—and he had a nostalgic regard for the faith that was linked with ancient churches, age-old country life, and moral ideals—but the content, if not the manner, of his philosophical poems reminds us of his more exotic predecessors. Though most of his poetry came much later (1898-1928), the essence of his view of life, the endurance of 'Crass Casualty', was set forth in the sonnet *Hap* of 1866, the year of *Poems and Ballads* (and of De Tabley's stoic

Philoctetes) and the year after *Atalanta*. And while
Hardy here dissociated himself from vain defiance of
the gods, his fatalism—or whatever we wish to call
it—remained very much that of Swinburne and
FitzGerald, as the last paragraph of *Tess* or, as
we observed above, the last chorus of *The Dynasts*
sufficiently indicates. But if Hardy's philosophy was
simple, his brooding compassion was large. He saw
nature as a congeries of living and lifeless things
emptied of order and purpose, the work perhaps of a
Godhead dying downwards, a Vast Imbecility, and
yet a world in which beauty may flower out of chaos
and pain and in which man endures with the process
of the seasons.

In contrast with Meredith's swift, elliptical
energy, his mighty opposite often writes like a man
who has just become articulate. He has his moments
of subdued ecstasy, that bring with them a lyrical
note, but in general he seems to be feeling his way
through the puzzles and tragedies of life and feeling
his way through language and rhythm at the same
time. Since he was a tireless experimenter in verse
forms, we may assume that all his effects were deliberate. Set against the Keats-Tennyson tradition,
Hardy (a partial disciple of William Barnes) is
homely, prosaic, gnarled, and sometimes odd. But
even awkwardness is an element in his rugged
honesty. A great many of his poems, it must be said,
are slight and unrewarding; some—not always those
made most familiar by anthologies—have a sombre
rightness and power. *The Darkling Thrush, Drum-
mer Hodge,* and *In Time of 'the Breaking of Nations'*
might be compared, by the way, with the first two
lyrics of *A Shropshire Lad* and the *Epitaph on an*

Army of Mercenaries. To add one futile sentence, neither Hardy's miscellaneous verse nor his novels would have prepared us for the largeness of vision that sustains *The Dynasts.* And the size and the date (1903–8) of *The Dynasts* prompt a no less futile reference to the mammoth epics of that isolated figure, Charles Doughty, who is much better known for his Arabian travels.

Hardy presents the phenomenon of a novelist returning, in his old age, to poetry and becoming one of the leaders of young poets, poets who were trying to shake off moribund Pre-Raphaelitism and get a fresh start. In our hostile retrospect, Georgian poetry has become identified with mildly ecstatic pottering about English lanes and hedgerows, but a number of the writers included in Sir Edward Marsh's anthologies (1911–22) do not altogether bear out that notion and are too diverse to be summarily labelled. Some names must serve as shorthand, instead of comments. Poets who appeared in both the first and the last volumes (and in most of the others as well) were Lascelles Abercrombie, W. H. Davies, Walter de la Mare, John Drinkwater, W. W. Gibson, D. H. Lawrence, and Harold Monro; in the first but not in the last were Gordon Bottomley, Rupert Brooke (d. 1915), G. K. Chesterton, James Elroy Flecker (d. 1915), John Masefield, Sturge Moore, and James Stephens; and among newer names in the last were Edmund Blunden, Robert Graves, Richard Hughes, Peter Quennell, V. Sackville-West, and J. C. Squire. Intervening volumes had included some of these and such others as Ralph Hodgson and Siegfried Sassoon, and one piece by Isaac Rosenberg, whose best work appeared after his death in France in 1918. Edward

Thomas and Wilfred Owen (killed in France in 1917 and 1918), Laurence Binyon, Yeats, and the much older but productive veteran Hardy, and the rising Imagists, did not appear at all. Some of the Georgians do reflect a very English world of rural peace and security, a world untroubled by the outward and inward problems that oppressed Hardy and, in more modern ways, Yeats and Lawrence. Of the poetry of rural reflection, probably Mr. Blunden's, which is not merely that, has worn the best, because of a concreteness of observation and language that are both authentic and artistic. For all its unpretentious freshness and variety, much Georgian verse had by no means got rid of Pre-Raphaelite romanticism and rhetoric. Rupert Brooke's *Dust*, for instance, was a dilution of Donne's *The Ecstasy* in which intensity was attained through phrases like 'your swift hair'. We prefer the very Georgian, and charming, *Old Vicarage, Grantchester*.

A number of writers were hardly Georgian except in time, and not always in that. Sturge Moore (1870–1944), whose first volume had appeared in 1899, was a direct heir of the Pre-Raphaelites, but he had an aesthetic and ethical philosophy, and his pictorial instinct went along with an individual density of style. Mr. Masefield (1878–   ) had begun with the Kiplingesque *Salt Water Ballads* (1902), and in 1911 he fluttered the polite world with the lurid violence of *The Everlasting Mercy*. His ties with the past continued to reveal themselves both in tales of action and in apostrophes to Beauty; the two strains were merged in the stirring *Dauber* (1913). At the opposite pole from Mr. Masefield's rather slipshod muse was the delicate art of Mr. de la Mare (1873–   ),

whose moonlight enchantments are not merely a
withdrawal from a scientific world but create a
world of imagination beyond the limits of the visible;
and his latest meditations on life and time (1950–1)
are a ripe testament of serenity not won by escape.
Edward Thomas (1878–1917), with his blend of
nature and reflection, might seem at first glance to
be only another Georgian, but for him the substantial beauties of the rural scene were only a partial
insurance against a modern mind's consciousness of
loss and negation. Rupert Brooke (1887–1915) had
become something of a legend even before his death
in Scyros; his sonnets on the war, the last echoes,
so to speak, of Henley's *England, my England,* were
soon submerged in the anti-heroic bitterness of
Sassoon and others. By far the most important of the
war poets was Wilfred Owen (1893–1918)—a late
and fervent disciple of Keats—whose work had a
deeper note than anger, and whose art helped to
inaugurate the modern movement. And before and
during the war other poets had been charting new
directions.

CHAPTER VI

THE MODERN PERIOD

T W O world wars and their consequences, and anticipation of a more terrible third one, make up the
history of the period 1914–52 and the experience, in
some degree, of all individuals who have lived
through all or part of those years or of the many
who were killed. But even if there had been no
wars, the modern poet would have found himself
in a situation much more difficult than confronted
his predecessors. The reasons have become a set
of clichés, though they are clichés of oppressive,
even paralysing, actuality. Many of the spectres
that have haunted this generation are, directly or
indirectly, the offspring of science, not merely new
weapons of mass-destruction but more insidious,
everyday enemies of traditional order and security—
the decay of religious faith and of moral values, the
predominance of a purely naturalistic view of life
and man, the mechanization of both external
existence and the individual personality, the change
from communal stability to the urban atomizing
of society, and so on.

These dislocating and dehumanizing forces were,
to be sure, in operation long before our time, and
they have been encountered in earlier chapters, but
in the last thirty or forty years their momentum has
been greatly accelerated, their impact greatly
widened. The modern literary and philosophical
scene includes, along with confident children of the

empirical fact, a good many conservatives and repentant liberals, and the work of the chief poets and many lesser ones has been in some form a revolt against a desiccating scientific positivism. Modern rebels, however, and modern poets in general, have, with a very few exceptions, been cut off by science from some central supports and themes of earlier poets. Those earlier poets, from Spenser, Donne, and Milton onward, had abundant occasion for despair, yet, when we think of the high religious, metaphysical, and ethical faith that sustained men of the Renaissance, or of the more secular but still invincible idealism of the romantic poets, it might well seem—whatever the necessity of accepting science and its results—as if ours is a world of hollow men, emptiness within contemplating emptiness without. And while this has been a common loss, the poet especially has had further problems, whether old and intensified or relatively new—the pressure of world events that dwarf the helpless individual, the alternatives of contemplative detachment or social responsibility, the lack of communal tradition and experience which the poet can share and use, the extinction of 'myth' and 'ritual' in our rationalistic and mechanized world, the difficulties of expression and communication in an age of disintegrated and vulgarized culture. In short, since poetry must be an act of faith, for both the poet and the reader, what kind of integration or affirmation or response can be achieved in a time of radical scepticism, confusion, anxiety, and fear?

The reactions to such problems, or some of them, that came from Hardy and Housman have been touched upon already. Another voice from the past was that of the aged Robert Bridges (1844–1930), whose Pre-Raphaelitism, disciplined by an austere taste, had earlier yielded many short poems of delicate refinement. But *The Testament of Beauty* (1929), an ambitious attempt to fuse naturalism with idealism, was not a satisfying affirmative *De Rerum Natura* for our age; if Santayana was his Epicurus, Bridges was no Lucretius. Nor was the poem a modern *In Memoriam*; whereas Tennyson had had to overcome stark despair, Bridges had not, and the aloof serenity and preciosity of his versified treatise seemed to belong to a noble but not quite real world.

Even before the First World War new impulses had begun to work in poetry and criticism, and several movements were forwarded by the dynamic, erratic, and flamboyant Ezra Pound (1885–   ). One movement was Imagism, which early enlisted the crusading energies of Mr. Pound and Amy Lowell, and which attracted a good many of the younger writers, English and American. But Imagist verse has not worn very well. Concentration on clear-cut images and the virtual excluding of traditional reflection were an effort to strike through the soft haze of deliquescent romanticism, and the movement did help to sharpen perception and phrasing and eliminate emotional vagueness. However, it attacked symptoms rather than the disease, and was a theory of technique rather than a theory of poetry; the Imagists on the whole had little to say, and the hard bright surfaces they saw were not enough. Imagism also helped to break down merely conventional metrics and allowed poets to write a poem as it came, to let theme and mood take their natural shape. Such emancipation was no doubt a good thing, though it encouraged an amount of lazy sprawling that was not poetry by any definition. The chief modern poets, Yeats, Mr. Eliot, and others, have combined liberty with rigorous discipline, and their powerful and individual rhythms are very far from polyphonic or chopped prose.

The Georgian anthologies were not fully representative of the years 1911–22, and typical Georgian verse came to look more like a mild eddy than a main current. Perhaps the quickest way of indicating the emergence of 'modern' poetry from a transitional mixture of old and new is to recall some publications of the years 1917–22. Along with books from a dozen or more orthodox Georgians, there were: T. S. Eliot's *Prufrock* (1917), which may be said to have inaugurated modern poetry; the *Poems* (1918) of Gerard Manley Hopkins (d. 1889), which were to electrify many of the younger writers; the *Poems* (1920) of Wilfred Owen (killed in 1918), which were to have a more 'prosaic' and astringent effect; several volumes from the unwearied Hardy, whose prosaic astringency had long been working on his juniors; several volumes from the tormented romantic, D. H. Lawrence (1885–1930), who, loathing the scientific intellect and all its works, sought salvation in the reality of animal energies and sex, and whose 'vitalist' gospel was to fortify a number of younger poets; several transitional volumes from the now converted or modernized romantic, Yeats; and volumes from the not readily classifiable Siegfried Sassoon, Robert Graves, Aldous Huxley, and the Sitwells. Then in 1922 came two works in prose and verse that were to make this year a landmark in modern literature, *Ulysses* and *The Waste Land*, although they were not at first received with general understanding and acclamation.

All these names carry their significance, and some other names and titles will help to define the spirit and direction of these and later years. Sir Herbert Grierson's *Metaphysical Lyrics and Poems of the Seventeenth Century* (1921) made Donne and his fellows better known among the literati than they had been. Poetic taste and practice were radically affected by the critical doctrines of T. E. Hulme (killed in 1917), T. S. Eliot (*The Sacred Wood*, 1920), I. A. Richards (*Principles of Literary Criticism*, 1924), and their rapidly growing band of disciples. *The Criterion* (1922–39), edited by Mr. Eliot, and *Scrutiny* (1932–53), edited by Dr. F. R. Leavis, were the chief periodical media for the new criticism, which was intellectual, precisely analytical, and anti-romantic. Hostility to the romantic tradition was a conspicuous strain in the new movement, whether or not it could be justly called a new kind of classicism. For nearly a century the romantic poets had been virtually the ideal and definition of non-dramatic poetry, for critics as well as general readers. Now they were roughly dethroned and replaced by Donne and his school; linked with these were the supreme exemplars of 'good' writing, Dante and Shakespeare. The new criteria were often applied with arbitrary and uncritical dogmatism; the canonization of Donne brought with it the excommunication not only of most romantic and Victorian poets but of Milton. There was, however, a very positive value in the rediscovery of a body of poetry that seemed a unique answer to the poetical needs of our time. Metaphysical colloquialism of style and rhythm, realistic particularity, toughness of sensibility, the complex and often dissonant expression of tension and conflict, the resources of irony, ambiguity, paradox, and wit—such qualities helped to energize and tighten the modern temper and technique, to create an attitude and a medium suited to a troubled, sceptical, anti-heroic age.

There are of course reservations to be made about the metaphysical revival, and there were other influences at work, from the French Symbolists to the rhythms of the internal-combustion engine. While serious modern poetry is obviously far more colloquial than nineteenth-century poetry normally was, it has—like Donne's—its own rhetoric, and can be quite as literary and unnatural as any previous poetic idiom; it might be asked, moreover, on what grounds colloquialism can be set up as an exclusive poetic absolute. And some main characteristics of modern technique may be partly attributed to both the scientific findings and the moral confusion of our time. Elliptical discontinuity is related to psychology's account of mental processes, conscious and unconscious, and also to modern ideas of discontinuity in nature (as contrasted with the rigorous law of nineteenth-century science). Poets, whether themselves distrusting traditional values and verities, or aware of general distrust, have been driven back to the irrefragable truth of concrete particulars and the data and symbols of private experience. Overt reflection and affirmation, in the past the products of relative assurance, have been either drastically limited in scope or replaced or enveloped by the oblique and non-committal and ironical. Then modern poems are likely to develop around and through images, instead of having a 'logical' structure of ideas. Thus, unlike most earlier poetry, a modern poem may seem to be, in a sense, only half-written; much more is left to be done by the reader, and interpretation may (in the useful phrase of Sir Thomas Browne) admit a wide solution. Modern poets have often been accused of being excessively and wilfully difficult, but the same charge was lodged in earlier periods against poets who have long been acquitted; and time can always be relied upon to distinguish between authentic, inevitable obscurity and mere fashion. It might be added that there is a parallel difference between authentic and merely fashionable 'despair'.

In these few pages we can, as usual, look only, and briefly, at a few conspicuous and representative figures and tendencies.

Mr. Pound, the brash Western invader of England and Europe, comes into this sketch for a moment as a destructive and creative influence. He might be labelled a sort of romantic anti-romantic. He began as an heir of the recent past, of both aestheticism and Browning, and he posed against a façade of variegated and exotic culture, Chinese, Latin, Italian, Provençal. Probably not many of his short poems claim a high place in our memories, and critics are not agreed on the proportion of poetry embedded in the ever-multiplying *Cantos*, but no one would dispute Pound's importance as a poetic trail-blazer and tool-maker. Abjuring violently the 'poetical' post-romantic legacy, he was a pioneer labourer in the fashioning of a poetic language and rhythm based on common speech.

W. B. Yeats (1865–1939) was in some ways an independent, self-sufficient explorer, not aligned, at least in his full maturity, with current fashions and social creeds. But he also exemplified in some ways the problems and the evolution of modern poetry. In the late 1880's, in association with Morris, Wilde, Lionel Johnson, Dowson, Arthur Symons, and other members of the Rhymers' Club, Yeats was a disciple of Rossetti and Pater and Pre-Raphaelite aestheticism, a sort of Irish Morris, weaving into Celtic legend the soft threads of 'poetical' beauty. In *The Green Helmet* (1910), and more clearly in *Responsibilities* (1914) and later volumes, we see the aesthete of the Celtic twilight becoming a poet of the troubled Irish present and, more largely and simply, a poet. From first to last he had in his head Irish characters and folk-lore, on his tongue the language and rhythms of Irish speech, and, as he became more and more himself, he shed his coat of mythological embroidery for a colloquial but ceremonial nakedness, a precision, strength, and symbolic density all his own. The richest fruit of Yeats's second growth came in *The Tower* (1928), *The Winding Stair* (1933), and some pieces in *Last Poems* (1940). He had moved from the rank and file to the head of the procession, to become, most people would say, the greatest of modern poets, and to exert a potent influence upon all younger writers who could absorb it.

Various external and internal causes had combined to change a dreamer of lovely dreams into a major poet—the general process of ripening, the experience of love, writing for the stage, the kindling of nationalistic ardour in the fire of the Irish rebellion, and heterogeneous spiritual and literary influences from Plato and Plotinus to Berkeley and Blake, from Donne to the Symbolists and Pound. And there was his own wrestling with problems of art and life. 'We begin to live when we have conceived life as tragedy.' A man of religious instincts, who had been deprived of traditional faith by Darwin and Tyndall, Yeats revolted, like Blake and others, against the 'Grey Truth' of scientific rationalism. What he craved was a unity of being provided by a unified culture. And, like Blake, Yeats saw the disintegration of culture and of the human personality as beginning in the later seventeenth century, in the idea of man's passivity before a mechanized nature as opposed to impassioned contemplation of a reality that was both logical and boundless. One clue to his direction is his setting up, against Locke, of Henry More, the Cambridge Platonist, and the Platonic conception of the World-Soul. But whereas More's and earlier ages had inherited a traditional framework of belief and thought, the 'unchristened' Yeats—again like Blake —had to make his own, out of scattered fragments of mystical and occult lore. A reader who began with Yeats's exposition of his system, *A Vision* (1925–37), might be pardoned for doubting if substantial poetry could spring from such a strange and elaborate construction of 'Platonic' cycles of cultural and individual life. Yet, though Yeats's finest writing casts its spell even if its 'meaning' is dimly apprehended, the materials of the *Vision*—filtered down through the critics—do furnish essential understanding and enrichment of the poet's symbols, Babylon, Byzantium, the moon, 'The Second Coming', and the rest.

Yeats's greatest poems have to do with the most central of all tensions, the claims of the flesh and the spirit, the temporal and the eternal, the Many and the One. The pagan poet, hating abstractions and restraints, would feel the pride of life, the raptures and pangs of the natural man; yet his soul would escape from the fury and mire of human veins into the starlit dome, from bondage to a dying animal into the artifice of eternity. And both impulses were quickened by the sense of oncoming age, the fear of withering into truth and wisdom. At times, as in *Sailing to Byzantium*, Yeats can turn with relative serenity from the flux of life to the ideal of enduring art. At other times, the poet who could mock Plotinus' thought and cry in Plato's teeth was able to identify the One with the Many, to rejoice, as in *Among School Children*, in the contemplation of man as a part of nature, or the harmonious unity of all being. Or, in that tremendous sonnet, *Leda and the Swan*, the animal, the human, and the supernatural are fused in one mythical, actual, and prophetic moment, a pagan parallel, in Yeats's gospel, to the Annunciation. Yet it may be said that his experience of these tensions is more violent than profound, because his poles are too simply aesthetic and barbaric. His language and rhythms have become a powerful and magical blend of simplicity, complexity, and splendour, but the man does not seem to have attained the maturity of the artist. If we think of the young Keats, who, with similar unresolved tensions, had a warm humanity, a growing ethical and spiritual wisdom, we may wish that age had brought to a great poet a creed less devoted to the glorification of mere animal vitality. The partly parallel creed of Lawrence—who also lacked physical vigour—was at least a positive faith, however misguided or inadequate; in Yeats, apparently, the vacuum left by a mainly aesthetic view of life was open to waves of lust and rage.

T. S. Eliot was born in St. Louis in 1888, some months after the death of Matthew Arnold, and, stretching Pythagorean (or Yeatsian) doctrine, we might think of him as a partial reincarnation. He arrived, at an early age, at a position of much more oracular authority—among the literary intelligentsia—than Arnold ever enjoyed, and had a far stronger and more immediate influence upon the poetry, criticism, and taste of his period. While in both men there are gaps or antinomies between the poet and the critic, Mr. Eliot's critical theory has more closely accompanied and explained his poetry. The differences between his poetry and criticism and Arnold's are perhaps more obvious than the resemblances, yet Mr. Eliot could call himself a classicist, and the cosmopolitan outlook that was distinctive in Arnold has been distinctive in his successor. It was the American who, along with his more volatile countryman, Mr. Pound, freed English poetry from the provincialism it had fallen into and reunited it with the main stream of the European tradition.

Yeats of course had tapped that tradition at many points, but many of those points were peripheral or subterranean. Though Mr. Eliot has been hardly less eclectic and exclusive in his self-education, the cultural matrix of his poetry has been composed mainly of orthodox materials, and the result has been an orthodox as well as individual whole. Some of the formative influences on his thought and

technique were Irving Babbitt, T. E. Hulme, and
Mr. Pound; Dante; Shakespeare and other Elizabethan dramatists; Donne and other metaphysicals;
and such French poets as Gautier, Baudelaire, and
Laforgue. There have been many others of importance, such as *The Golden Bough* and the *Bhagavad-
Gita*, the Bible and the liturgy, Lancelot Andrewes
and St. John of the Cross. And Mr. Eliot is one of
those highly literary poets who get some of their
most original effects from echoing other writers. In
Sweeney among the Nightingales, for example, the
sinister references to the circles of the stormy moon,
the Virgilian hornèd gate, and gloomy Orion
apparently come from Marlowe's *Doctor Faustus*.
In Mr. Eliot's early poems the heroic symbols of an
older day commonly become ironical, either through
a deliberate twist or through remaining heroic in a
debased context. (The half-concealed allusion is
not, by the way, a modern invention; it was effectively
used by Spenser and Milton.)

Most of Mr. Eliot's earlier poetry was a report,
dryly and even lightly satirical, but serious, on the
sick and dying civilization he saw, a series of contrasts
—arresting if unhistorical—between an ideal heroic
past and an ugly unheroic present. Just as Arnold
turned from the confused, empty busyness of his
age to the fresh, simple rightness of feeling that he
found in the primitive Biblical and classical worlds,
so Eliot turned back from the physical and spiritual
squalor of the modern city, whether in its 'arty'
drawing-rooms or dingy streets and lodgings, to
times of spiritual health and fullness of life. But
instead of Arnold's direct statement and reflection he
used the shock tactics of an age of speed and the

cinema—objective recital of particulars, sharply juxtaposed pictures of the actual and the ideal, anecdotes of mordant irony and understatement, and wit of Latinized edge. The poet might be an invisible spectator or, as in *The Love Song of J. Alfred Prufrock*, merged with the speaker. That inspired title announces an unheroic theme; Lancelot and Tristram have given place to a timid, self-conscious suburbanite who has measured out his life with coffee spoons. But the speaker is also a metaphysical poet who can get outside and criticize himself, and a Jamesian New-Englander who would break loose from his Puritan tradition. The notorious opening image, of the evening spread out against the sky 'Like a patient etherised upon a table'—a great change from, say, 'The holy time is quiet as a Nun Breathless with adoration'—applies to more than the evening; and at the end the mermaids or sirens, who ever since Homer had meant sensual seduction from the heroic life, have become symbols of heroic emancipation and fulfilment.

In *Poems* (1920), *The Waste Land* (1922), and *The Hollow Men* (1925), the same technique is exploited, with more complete assurance and richer density (perhaps an excess in *The Waste Land*). Whether in deceptively simple quatrains or in free verse of very individual suppleness and timbre, Mr. Eliot is a superlatively adroit or inspired master of language and rhythm. Not a great many English poets have had such economical, subtle, and magical power over word and sound and symbol. The nightingales singing near the Convent of the Sacred Heart call up the two great traditions of Western man, the classical and the Christian, and become a judgment not only on the gross Sweeney and his enemies but on the modern world—not without the further implication that the world has always been evil. All these poems, short and long, were pictures of rootless, restless human beings dehumanized by a Godless, mechanized, and sterile civilization. But Mr. Eliot was much more than he was often taken to be in the 1920's, the voice of post-war defeatism or the satirist of European decadence. To the pictures of boredom and horror the longer poems added gleams of possible glory; *Gerontion, The Waste Land,* and *The Hollow Men*—and the 'Ariel Poems'— revealed a positive theme, the way of religious salvation. A religious 'message', however, could hardly stir the modern reader except through a flank attack. Everyday speech and slang, the brittle, staccato rhythms of the modern city, are mixed with the exalted language and symbols and the slow, weighted, broken utterance of an agonized religious vision. As in earlier poems, there is almost no comment or connective tissue; objective particulars, crude or glamorous, carry their multiple suggestions of drought and fertility, present and past, lust and love, pride and humility, sin and redemption.

If *The Waste Land* was Mr. Eliot's *Inferno, Ash Wednesday* (1930) and *Four Quartets* (1943) were his *Purgatorio* and `Paradiso*. In *Ash Wednesday* the poet's vision is turned inward; the ugliness of urban civilization is blotted out, and the strain and stress of religious conversion are rendered through Dantesque symbols and images of nature. *Four Quartets*, poems bound together by parallels and variations in structure and theme and the symbolic use of the old 'four elements', embody and explore

further phases of religious experience. The central
subject is the effort of the individual soul to 'redeem
the time', to rise above the flux of life and circum-
stance to full spiritual integration. 'The world' is
present, as symbol and background, in English
and American scenes of historical or personal
memory, and images range from the rose-garden to
the brown Mississippi, from ancient rural peace to
the time-ridden faces in the Underground and an
air-raid; but satire has been replaced by compassion,
and the poems are half-private, half-public religious
exercises. Experience in writing for the stage may
have contributed, as with Yeats, to the moulding
of the poet's later manner. Difficulty remains, in
both elusive symbols and abstractions, but particulars merge with reflection, and the language and
rhythm move from the level of mystical meditation
and lyrical incantation to the deliberately prosaic.
In general, Mr. Eliot's development has carried him
farther and farther away from both conventional
liberalism and poetry of concrete immediacy, and
his later work has been both deplored and acclaimed.
At any rate his religious and artistic evolution has
attested his integrity. And scarcely any English
poet has produced less surplusage; almost every line
he has written has been 'important'.

If Edith Sitwell (1887–   ) has not attained the
dominant position and influence of Yeats and Mr.
Eliot, her evolution has been akin to theirs. From
the start she possessed a highly original sensibility
and craftsmanship. The poems written during and
after the First World War created or re-created a
beautiful private world, aristocratic and romantic,
bucolic and bizarre. Some of the early poems might

have been the work of a Christina Rossetti—the
Christina Rossetti of *Goblin Market*—who had grown
up in the refinement and confinement of the era
described in Sir Osbert Sitwell's autobiography, and
who had read seventeenth-century and modern
writers and learned to convey both wit and emotion
in hard, sharp images. In that partly fairy-tale
world, childhood memories and dreams and people
and the creatures and things of nature, homely and
real or bookish and exotic, were contemplated under
both the bright sun and the traditional shadows of
time and death. But the pervading sense of loss
embraced more than a vanished childhood. Like
Mr. Eliot, Miss Sitwell had her primitivist or ideal
vision of a past when God walked in the gardens,
when man and life had strength and warmth and
wholeness of being. But, unlike Mr. Eliot's dry-point
etchings of mean streets and mean souls, of corruption with a cosmopolitan veneer, of emptiness and
sterility, the small, richly coloured world of Miss
Sitwell's earlier poems allowed only glimpses of an
outer civilization in decay. In *Gold Coast Customs*
(1929) she moved in Mr. Eliot's direction, into poetry
of the public and brutal world. She had already
pictured, in such lines as these from *Troy Park* (1925),
the same waste land, the same hollow men:

> *This is my hell; not even fear to keep . . .*
> *So trivial is that hell, no devils weep*
> *Therein; but the maimed dwarfs of this poor*
> *life,—*
> *Terrible straining mechanisms, crouching*
> *In trivial sands, with laughter like stones*
> *tumbling*
> *They watch, rejoicing at the giants crumbling.*

Like Mr. Eliot too, but in her own way, Miss Sitwell suggests the loss, in our mechanized age, of an older idealism and assured belief through ironic echoes of the Elizabethans—'Then die with me and be my love' (*Serenade: Any Man to Any Woman*); 'But steel wings fan thee to thy rest' (*Lullaby*). In her latest writing, such as *Three Poems of the Atomic Age* and *The Song of the Cold*, the fact of hell, the ultimate cold in the heart of fallen man, are central, and, while the poet's early preoccupation with time and death and love and rebirth continues, these ideas and symbols have now a positively religious depth and force and austerity. There is still little actual contemporary reference, such as Eliot and younger poets use, but abstract images, marshalled in long, sweeping lines, express a vision of prophetic and compassionate intensity and elevation. Critical opinion, however, is not unanimous on the 'genuineness' of Miss Sitwell's poetry.

In the 1930's the established poets continued to be more or less productive, both the traditionalists and the eminent modernists whom we have just glanced at, but the chief phenomenon was the emergence of a much younger group who were quickly hailed as the leaders of a new movement. C. Day Lewis, W. H. Auden, Louis MacNeice, and Stephen Spender, who were born in the years 1904–9, were for some time united by similarity of background and outlook and by personal ties. These and other poets belonged to the generation that came to maturity in the post-war period of exhaustion, economic depression, defeatism, pacifism, and general confusion and revolt. Many writers of that generation saw a possible alternative to despair in the hopes for man kindled by popular revolutions, and some lost their lives in Spain. And then came the Second World War, in which all England was a fighting front, and which darkened still further the already dark world of the poets.

If the poetry of the decade had any one dominant motive, it was an acute social consciousness, with a strong infusion of rebellious and divided self-consciousness. In addition to the general evidence in the poetry, there are such special testimonies as Mr. Lewis's *Transitional Poem* (1929) and *The Magnetic Mountain* (1933), Mr. MacNeice's *Autumn Journal* (a product of the time of Munich), and Mr. Auden's *New Year Letter* (1941). Mr. Spender, whose poems, though reflecting a sick age, have been especially and earnestly concerned with self-integration, has provided the fullest document in his minute, candid, and tormented autobiography, *World within World* (1951). For young men who had grown up in what had been a solid if stuffy society, all things, including themselves, had got out of joint; conventional beliefs and ideals and old-school slogans were either shattered or abominably alive; and nothing seemed substantial except what was abhorrent, nothing clear or strong except the forces that submerged both the mass of people and individual integrity. It was a period of frustrated modern Hamlets, many of whom—to speak with no lack of sympathy—had a strain of Byron as well.

One might have expected a choir of Shelleys, but Shelley's revolutionary zeal was not enough to offset his romantic sensibility and manner, and Wilfred Owen, Eliot, and modern French poets had taught a technique of shifting focus and symbols, of satirical irony and toughness. Mr. Eliot, however, had contemplated the ugly world with detachment, and had lately seemed to withdraw from it altogether, and the younger men, though not indifferent to the timeless themes of poetry, saw a prior necessity of clearing away obstructions left over from a dead past. They had been immersed from birth in the actualities of the English and European scene, they were much more personal and topical in their utterance, and they carried colloquialism of allusion, language, and rhythm much farther than their elders. They carried it so far, indeed, that they sometimes approach versified journalism; they have attained rarely, if at all, the classical finality of Yeats and Mr. Eliot. Incessant outward and inward agitation allows few moments of repose. To make an old-fashioned kind of judgment (with which other readers might disagree), whereas many poems of Yeats and Eliot compel memorization, hardly anything of the younger poets' does. And, so far at any rate, we cannot point to any work by any one of the group as an indisputably major achievement. Their technical powers may be adequate or brilliant, but, like other people, they have been moving towards, rather than standing on, a firm centre of contemplation. At the least, however, their earlier poetry made confusion and malaise articulate, and they have been seeking a way out.

These four poets have gone through a partly parallel evolution and, though all have had their individual outlook and manner, there is some degree of sameness in their early arraignments of their class and cultural heritage, in their recitals of all the things in modern civilization that outraged young

intellectuals who were trying to break loose from
it. This body of writing is a vigorous and faithful—
if one-sided,—picture of a world in decay, yet in
retrospect it may have more historical than poetical
interest. The question was whether these poets had
the stamina not only to repudiate a hateful and
guilty past and present but to gain a more positive
vision and foundation for the future. While Mr.
Auden has taken a religious direction, Messrs.
Lewis, Spender, and MacNeice have remained, or
become, subdued liberals of a less militant kind.
They have discovered grounds of faith and hope,
limited but relatively sure, where men have found
them before, in individual integrity and courage
and love and in nature. However significant their
'revolutionary' writing, their poems, early or late,
that exist most fully and securely as poetry are
probably those slighter pieces in which angry
reporting has given place to a richer density of
suggestion, to quiet evocations of cherished scenes
and moments, to distilled meditations on time and
life and death, to warm recognition of everyday
humanity.

These general remarks are roughly applicable to
the common elements in the four poets and a
number of their contemporaries. We can look a
little more closely at only one representative,
Mr. Auden (1907–   ), who moved to the United
States in 1939. Much of his writing, and of his
fellows', might be comprehended under one of his
later titles, *The Age of Anxiety*. His development,
except in its latest phase, has been typical of his
generation, of its efforts to find a creed that would
fill the modern spiritual void, that would reintegrate

fragmentary individuals and a fragmentary society. Against a civilization that was the work of empiric, economic man, the poet could appeal to youthful memories (the return to the womb, as some, including Mr. Auden, would say), to Marx, to Freud, to Kierkegaard. In *For the Time Being* (1944), a Christmas oratorio, Mr. Auden arrived, as some of his elders had, at a Christian standpoint (which some would call another version of the return to the womb). His conception of the difficult role of the modern poet is of course implicit in all his work, and it is made more explicit in the *New Year Letter*, the speech of Caliban in *The Sea and the Mirror*, and in the more or less notable poems on artists and thinkers, the elegies on Yeats, James, Freud, and Ernst Toller, and a number of other pieces on authors from Montaigne to Rimbaud; and the prose of *The Enchafèd Flood* (1950) creates a picture, in the romantic tradition, of the solitary Promethean explorer and builder. One brief statement is the wish (*September 1, 1939*) that the poet, composed like others of Eros and dust, may,

> Beleaguered by the same
> Negation and despair,
> Show an affirming flame.

It might perhaps be said that Mr. Auden is the cleverest poet since Pope, and the remark would be a tribute, with reservations; some readers are a little suspicious of technical virtuosity and fluency, especially when linked with intellectual and spiritual agility. At any rate Mr. Auden plays most of the instruments in the orchestra, and usually several at once. Metaphysical abstractions and newspaper immediacy, public events and private emotions, ominous prophecy and satirical clowning, the reality of evil and the need of love; modern ballads in the American vein and medieval alliterative verse; dimeters, trimeters, tetrameters, stanza-forms without number, and loose long lines and straight prose; dialectic and doggerel, lilting lyricism and dry irony, high rhetoric and flat undertones, poetical diction, scientific jargon, and the slang of the street—these and other ingredients bubble in Mr. Auden's pregnant pot (and, especially in his longer works, the alchemical process may be incomplete). Among the numerous attractive poems, a random example might be the one that opens the last full collection (1945), *Musée des Beaux Arts*, a short meditation in free verse which is casual, conversational, humorous, and poignant. However nimble and fertile his brain, Mr. Auden's best poetry generally springs from his comprehension of suffering, joy, love, and pity; a human and religious consciousness of a share in the world's guilt has added compassion to anger and disgust.

The work of this group was, at least in its beginnings, clearly definable. Since the later 1930's, however, there have been too many groups, splinter groups, and unattached individuals to make a pattern visible to the naked eye. Perhaps the most comprehensive label for some main tendencies of the 1940's is that which a number of writers, following Sir Herbert Read, inscribed on their banner, namely, 'romantic'. While that is not the most precisely helpful of words, it indicates a turning away from public and social commentary to various kinds of subjectivism or 'personalism'. This new romanticism

embodied a return to private experience and vision
and simple, natural things, but it could not, like the
original romantic movement, be called a 'renascence
of wonder'. The response to traditional themes
employed modern techniques and was toughened by
war and modern scientific scepticism; sometimes, on
the other hand, it was quickened by a religious or
semi-religious concern. While Sir Herbert Read—
and later I. A. Richards, a major critic turned poet—
allowed themselves only the bleak ecstasies of dis-
illusioned intellectuals, at the other end of the
romantic spectrum were such apocalyptic or Diony-
siac poets as the Irish George Barker (1913–   ) and
the Welsh Dylan Thomas (1914–53). Mr. Barker and
Thomas, however unlike each other, belong to the
'primitive' and 'mystical' tradition of Blake and
D. H. Lawrence, and at first a reader, baffled by a
welter of words and images, may be reminded (in a
non-political way) of 'The blind hysterics of the Celt'.
But the reader who perseveres may possibly recognize
in the fervid violence an effort to find meaning in or
beyond the immediate experience of love and
suffering and death. The world and the unconscious
self are not so much themes for reflection as myths
and metaphors to be felt. One may find both poets
most approachable in the more controlled moods in
which they are closest to actuality and yet transcend
it. Thomas's preoccupation with birth and rebirth
admits or demands a wealth of images from nature,
and his strange naked intensity of vision carries a
strange expressiveness—local if not total—of phrase
and rhythm.

But in these last decades poetry, while abundant
and competent, has in general been rather low-pulsed,

and it is difficult, at least in a few paragraphs, to mention outstanding or probably enduring or even representative names. Indeed some of the most distinctive poets do not seem to be representative, but rather timeless and individual voices—the metaphysical Edwin Muir (1887–1959), who was so preoccupied with time; or Robert Graves (1895–), whose poetry has not suffered from his sometimes boisterous and irresponsible prose; or the little-known Andrew Young (1885–), the quiet observer of nature. The unique John Betjeman (1906–) has risked his standing by being lively and popular; and Philip Larkin (1922–) has written at least one poem that is a contemporary classic. And a number of women have recorded their diverse but feminine reactions to the universal problems of living in our world—Ruth Pitter, Kathleen Raine, Anne Ridler, Elizabeth Jennings.

We cannot end this sketch of recent English poetry without taking account of other nations outside England. Ireland or Eire has a sufficient and towering representative in Yeats, and a notable proportion of the newer poets are Welsh and Scottish. In the nations of the British Commonwealth, poetry has attained more or less maturity and modernity. Diverse representatives of South Africa—though they did not stay there—are Roy Campbell, William Plomer, and Charles Madge. Mr. Campbell's later and more sophisticated verse has not surpassed the swift exuberance of *The Flaming Terrapin* (1924). The Canadian E. J. Pratt (1883–), in *The Cachalot* (1925) and other narratives, heroic or satiric, displayed a primitive—though far from naïve—vitality of imagination and phrase somewhat akin to

Campbell's; and he combined a higher vision and a more austere art in *Brebeuf and His Brethren* (1940). The typical problem in Canada, and elsewhere, had been to break loose from English romanticism and achieve authenticity by becoming local and national without becoming provincial. Some of the older poets who reflected that process, or its successful completion, were the over-fluent Bliss Carman (1861–1929) and the more substantial Archibald Lampman (1861–99) and Duncan Campbell Scott (1862–1947); poets of the newest generations have been in full alliance with contemporary movements. Much the same things might be said of Australia and of such modern poets as Kenneth Slessor (1901–   ) and R. D. FitzGerald (1902–   ). The older Australian, W. J. Turner (1889–1946), we associate with English poetry; his real talent, visionary and intellectual, never reached quite satisfying fulfilment.

This sketch of the modern scene has included only some representative names, and even the next decade may greatly alter the perspective. In fifty years, when time has done its usual sifting (and if our world still exists and people are still writing and reading books), the position of some recent poets will, we may suppose, remain secure; and some others will have risen and others will have sunk. Since literary history is a warning against prophecies, we need not go beyond the safe prediction that, in the anthologies and criticism of A.D. 2000, the poetry of the years 1914–52 will present a picture that differs from ours. It has been said that that religion has the best chance of surviving which shall best succeed in fusing the temporal with the eternal, and the remark is no less true of poetry. Neither element by itself is enough, but the fusion, whatever form it takes, can endure.

Looking back over the poetry of six hundred years, we can hardly summarize in a page a book that has been in itself a meagre summary. The story is one of revolt turning into convention and of convention overthrown by a new revolt. Yet no convention or revolt—such as the classicism or romanticism of this last generation—has been very much like its predecessors, because the conditions are always changing. On a level beyond particular needs and aims, however, there has been a periodical and inevitable oscillation, both spiritual and technical, between classical and romantic poles. Modern poets, unhappily, have to a large degree lost real contact with the ancient classics, which throughout all former centuries were a main source of inspiration and of discipline, but the fundamental opposition is always there, between objectivity and subjectivity, between acceptance of established norms and rebellious individualism. Or perhaps it would be truer to say that the traditional individualism of the English genius has at times been restrained and tempered by ideals of discipline. As a rule, to repeat what was said at the beginning of this book, the greatest poets have been those who were not simply one thing or the other but who understood or contained within themselves the basic conflicts between order and disorder (not that such conflicts will make a great artist out of a small one).

The internal evolution of poetry has been profoundly affected by phenomena outside its own realm, above all by the steady change from religious faith to scientific naturalism, from belief in the world and man as constituting a divine order to belief in endless and inexplicable natural process. And along with that have gone other radical changes, ethical, psychological, social. The spiritual responsibilities of the poet have increased while the means of fulfilling them, in comparison with earlier resources, have been more and more limited, and while his audience has come to be a smaller and smaller proportion of the reading public. If the predicament of the modern artist is to be attributed mainly to the character of modern civilization, the poets have perhaps been not entirely blameless, and we must hope for fuller *rapprochement* between the poet and the common reader for the sake of both poetry and society. And while our civilization is predominantly scientific, now as in former times poetry can break through the tyranny of the positivist intellect and claim to be the breath and finer spirit of all knowledge. Finally, now as always, a central criterion of the major poet is his recognition of the unceasing conflict between good and evil.

INDEX

WITHDRAWN